This compilation is a labor of love, creative unrest, and the result of my need to add to the collective, artistic energy of the universe in written word. It's also meant to be a tangible show of appreciation for all the time, energy, blood, sweat, and tears spent on my behalf – by all of those in my life – to mold me into who and what I am today.

All of these poems are original works. The date of the final draft of this compiled, completed work was Saturday, October 4, 2014.

ISBN #978-1-312-57670-4

Cover art, book layout, and design by Michael DeBenedictis. Author picture taken by Amin Rahieem on Saturday, August 2, 2014.

NOTES

NOTES

All The Beautiful Shades of Grey

Of all the colors in the rainbow I'll take black and white
And by association grey
Of all the reasons in the world I'll use this one
I don't need to please you

Of all the people in the world whose opinions matter
Specifically to me
Of all the insignificant negative chatter
Is that all you have on me

For all the grief this sick and selfish world has given me
I think I feel like giving you a taste
For all the useless talk of politics and anti-matter
What has it ever done for you

Don't take me the wrong way
I really do care
I just care about the things that really matter

Don't take me the wrong way
I'm really not angry
I've just had all of the grief I'm going to take

Basquait

In a world on a string of the puppet master
In a state of collapse, on the verge of disaster
Should I move faster

In a city that doesn't remember your face
In a trance that every day is the same dance
Should I be prudent

When the words don't come is that a problem
Or the answer right in my face
When the stares get meaner and the people leave
Should I take it as a favor

In a house where the walls seems to script the story

In a time when the details are all too gory
Should I get out of here

I think I will
I think I might
I think I have to

In the mind of a man stuck in split decision
In the frame of broken glass, distorted mirror
Should I take another look to survive this night

March Or Reason

As the march for reason carries on
Are we gaining ground or losing step
As our eyes grow wider and vision dulls
Have we learned to lose what crumbles and falls

Have we learned the difference between our fates
What is will and what is selfish hate
As we reason God out of the picture
Does anybody notice the walls falling down

As we forget how fallible we are
As we grow rich and accept the bizarre
As perfectly normal, nothing out of place
Have we forgotten our own face

Have we learned nothing from our fall
Our souls need saved and the line
Drawn in the sand that we blew away
When we made idols today

This is what we call a march of reason
What we should ask is should we march or reason
This is what they call the season of demons
When we should fall onto our knees and try to seize them

Opus Of The Octopus-Armed Drummer

This is an ode to the man who can do it all

Sing it all, play it all, everything
This is in homage to greatest musician
The greatest in the whole wide world

This is an offering to the greater whole
The wider world, to taste what I bring
This is an invitation for the quiet ones
An invitation to stand up and sing

Four arms and legs, he'll get around to you
For means and ends, he'll explain it all to you
Two eyes and ears, he'll sense when you are near
Too wide-awake to sleep, he'll make the time for you

This is an ode to the greatest poet I've ever known
Who's ever droned and ever loaned
This is a reference to the wordsmith
With pencil marks on his paper chin

This is my contribution to the whole
To all who dream and think in scenes
This is the part I'll play in this fine game
The lives we lead are shared all the same

Crashed Philosophy

We hold the world with esteem for its ends and its means
Is it natural to think like a subhuman being
We see the mirror looking back with a smile or a frown
Is there time to really see what's all around us anyhow

Passing life in full view on the microscope tray
Tells a story, but does anyone listen anyway
Hear the beeps and ticks from the machines and clocks
Feel the beat and the pulse of this life's hard knocks

Is this for real or a real nice illusion
What do we know and can we say we do
Is there a ghost behind the wheel or the soundboard
Where is the vat of brains plugged in to the system

What's with the spirits in the trees or their fingers underground
Are they feeling their way to better places than down

Grand New Scheme

All of this, what a grand new scheme
Almost like an impossible dream
Nothing like anything used to be
Everything is so new and pristine

All of this just waiting for me
To tear it down, straight to the ground
Watch me work – it will only be a moment
Everything that you worked for is gone

All of this, what a great new game
Almost like there's nothing to fame
Get your face somewhere well-known quick
Do a dance – the people love schtick

All of this is way too easy
It's a joke and your street cred is shame
Show up once, do a trick for the masses
But make it quick, they all move so fast

I hope none of this is real, if it is it's such a shame
All the time and effort put into a wasted game
I hope none of this is real, just a sad illusion
It's not even bliss, there's no honor, when loyalty's dismissed

Head In The Radio

There's a head in the radio
Booming down from the satellites
Reaching out to the ghosts in machines
That secretly run everything

There's the men on my shoulders
One with horns and one with wings
There's the pattering sound of stampede
But I can't see anything

Over six million ants in line
Climbing, clambering, what a parade
All their mouths moving so fast
But they're not saying anything

All the colors and flashes on screen
Telling me just what I need
Don't they know they have no control
Over the voice that's guiding me

The head in the radio speaks, again
The impending rain is on its way
The ghost in the machine is alive, again
All the radio signals fade away

Young Man's Game

This is a young man's game, but sad to say
Only the old know the way to play
This a cosmic joke from the moment we're born
We're slowly dying our lives away

If this is how it has to be live just to breathe
If this is all there is to see let it be what we make it
If this is how it has to be live to be free
If this is all there is we might as well be the freaks

This is a loud man's place, but it's too bad
Only the quiet know what to say
This is an eternity's worth of riddles
If only we were up for the game

There's no time for begging or borrowing hours
There's no room for dragging and standing in line
There's no point in droning and talking for days
There's no word to say what hasn't been prayed

Forever's such a long, long time

Moleman

I'm the mole man and I'm living in a hole
With my headphones on and I don't where to go
From down here everything is unclear
I can't see ten feet ahead of me

All the blue skies just seem to turn pink
And the pink just turned into grey
I'm sure there's some significance to this
I just don't know what it is

Bob your head if you know what I just said
I don't have a clue – can you help me out, help me out
If you see something in front of me
Let me know where it is before I trip on it

All of this will be gone soon enough
Look around – see the matter breaking down
Brick by brick and cell by cell
It's falling apart all around you

From my vantage point under the ground
I'm under the sound and lost what I've found
So it won't matter any to me
When it all falls down around you

The Way You Intended

What you foresaw in your future
It obviously did not happen
What you once thought
It obviously did not come true

What we all wanted for today
It obviously was not meant to be
What we all wished for this moment
It obviously did not come to pass

It never turns out the way you intended
It's never remembered the way you mentioned
It's never recovered the way you suggested

It's never rejected the way you suppressed it

This is obviously not the way it was meant to happen

What you had put all your stock in
It obviously did not pay off
What you had put all your hope in
It obviously was the wrong bet to make

Temporal Thing One Of Many

I want to abandon words and reveries for the simple things
How can I turn out pages of words and oral histories
In such a fantastic game, it's all a pun that's no longer fun
Spun from romantic mills of the dreaming ones, the scheming sons

I want to take off and leave my place on ground behind
For better places and plains only reachable from the sky
In days where the climate changes everyday, in the worst ways
Spinning closer and closer to going down the drain

In dreams I can breathe, stop time, and take in the scenes
My anamnesis sets in and I can be anything
Free of the cranes and the chains they ascribe to be tied
Slip past the guards of the flies and lords of their wings

These are just temporal things, one of many, and then they're gone
Faded away out of life quick as they came, strayed just the same
All the names have been changed – so have the causes of shame
No more tricks from the hat and no waylaying at the gates

Peripatetic

I've got my feet on the ground and my head in the stars
Considered all the principles and all that's bizarre
I've taken into account what I've felt and what I've seen
All the intangible, fleeting things

I've come to trust in one thing and to do it this way
No matter what it does to me or what they all say
I've come to know myself best the only way that I can

Life is just a pursuit and wisdom comes on the move

Like a walking philosopher I'll make my mind as I go
Like a walking dead man I'll live for real, not for show

I've got my ear to the ground and my eyes ahead of me
Aware of what's on my mind, but it's waiting for the change
I'm going somewhere the lines don't exist
Where they've been blurred and the beaurocrats dismissed

I'm still aware of the spirits on my trail
A step ahead is all I need to be free
I've moved the mountains and parted the seas
That only served the devils behind me

I won't let you repeat your sin
You've killed another where I have been
I won't let you do what was done, again
And get away, you can't run

I won't go out of this alone
Even if it looks like you have won
I won't let reason lose the war
Let my life be the settling score

Space Kid

Your head is in the clouds, but promise me you won't come down
Your heart's dressed like a clown – see the words, don't hear the sound
You've spent your days away from here; just promise me you won't come back
It's not that I've grown tired of you; your ship will just get grounded way too soon

He's the son that we all know, he's known as the space kid
He goes places no one goes, forever will be the space kid

Your shoes are filled with sand from all the daydream trips and plans
Your heart is in your hands; don't give it up while you still stand
You've tripped the rift and lived to tell your story oh so well
Of all your ups and downs, of all your times in heaven and in hell

Calling all cars, calling all cars, we have a dreamer

Four foot nothing, brown hair, wearing a twirly-bird hat and two-tone suspenders
Suspect reported to be armed with a free mind, wait a minute
He appears to be skipping – he's skipping
Requesting back up, proceed with caution

Swan Song

If this is the last word that I ever say to you
Let it be strong, let it be pure, let it be true
If this is the first word that you've ever heard of mine
Then let it be a shame you've never heard before

Let this be my last try to reach the world
That never tried to reach back to me
Let this be the end of things as they are right now
I'll start walking down my own lost highway

When swans don't sing anymore
Everyone else loses their voice
When swans don't swim anymore
Everyone else loses their wings

90,811 Dreams

When I close my eyes I see the world
With brand new sight and eyes of pearl
There is no depth that I can't fall
There is no height that is too tall

I can dream in colors and black and white
I can stay awake and sleep all night
I can dream 90,811 dreams
Each one is different and still so real

White rabbits don't seem so strange at all
Red moons and stars that always fall
There is no myth that is not true
There are no lies and nothing to prove

Bring Me To My Knees

The first shots rang out and the war was on
Words flew in the wind and pride ran high
Hearts broke and silent voices spoke
Souls shook and stirred in the rising smoke

Lines in the sand dug into a trench
Guns took the place of love at hand
All at once man became a beast
Once hallowed grounds, the graves of the least

Is this way the way that we must live
Is this the only way to give
How can you be so callous
To feed the world your madness

There's so much more to life than this
We're racing to be disgraced
All of the good are dying
While you just keep on lying

The knife went deep and the damage was done
The final straw was burned up like the sun
In a passionate moment the line was crossed
There's no going back now – the war has been lost

The house was divided and swept away
Split down the middle with nothing to say
The innocent left by the side of the road
They all know what happened, but can't speak a word

In the aftermath what was left
All of the lines are drawn in the sand
Now the foundation has been cracked
The pieces too far gone to be put back

In This World

When the angels themselves are crying out in protest
Is it enough for you to see you're not the only one
Who sees a flaw in this scheme, the world that we live in
That teaches ideals and dreams, but only turns out victims

Where is the justice in this world
Where is the truth, has it been sold

In the last valiant stand the hero was the target
At the sad, unfair hands of a much less honest system
It didn't matter what he did, he was set up just to lose
All the valor and might didn't matter when it all went down

Where is the justice in this world
Where are the righteous – were they too bold

Are you running away from what waits for you tomorrow
Can you feel everything, all the slings and arrows

Indie Rock Casual

I can see you in that red leather jacket
With a scarf around your neck and those snake skin boots
With a whole lot of style that's gone unappreciated
A whole lot of style that's gone unappreciated

I can you with that custom-made Gibson
And a classic blues amp with a wah wah pedal
With a whole lot of sounds in that pedal board box
A whole lot of sounds in that pedal board box

You're the image of the classic indie rocker
With a smooth attitude and no guts, no glory
With your attitude
With your attitude

You're the poster child of this generation
With a dream in his hands in crumbles in pieces
But it's not your fault
It's the way this world treats everyone, anymore

I can see you on that mid-size tour bus
That gets you here to there with no bother, no fuss
With your focus on the music as your legacy
Your focus on the music as your legacy

I see your picture on the album cover
With a cigarette hanging out of your mouth
You're the casual man among the mothers
Who didn't want much, he just wanted enough

Love Is Lost On Them

Though love is lost on all of them don't ever forget it's in your hands
Those feelings are oh so strange to them; don't give your heart and soul away
This world is not a place for us; all of us who have a heart that breaks
This time is all so wrong for us; all of us who need the time to recover

Though they will pass their guilt on you, don't take it even if it's free
It's just not natural for them to feel, don't let them make you feel strange
Though it may seem the clock won't stop don't be afraid to step aside
Time won't stand still for anyone, don't let it push you on ahead

Though pains of life may stretch another don't bend until you break
Float on against the tide and see you don't need to give an explanation

Love is lost on them; their hearts are cold, misused and sold
Tired souls attract the tired, weary, skeptic fools
Love is lost on them; their eyes are covered from both sides
When you can't see what's all around you what's the use of sight

Love is lost on them theirs' is not understanding
There is no connection from their heart into their soul
Love is lost on them; theirs' is not true conviction
No meanings underscore their steps – their steps don't leave a trail

Pieces On The Floor

You fell to far to ever get back up again
You missed the mark, the chance will never come again
You aimed too high and hit ground the hardest this time
You never felt this low before

They took your wind; your sails are all but useless now
They shook you up; you're cracked and broken in
They locked you out and didn't give you any keys

They shut you down forever

We're nothing but pieces on the floor
Wrecked ships left over from the storm
There's nothing left to pick up now
It's all been destroyed this time for good

It never used to be like this, people used to care
It wasn't meant to be this way; why are we not scared
It doesn't have to end this way; we've got two legs to stand on
It should have never gone this far, now who's left to blame

The world has never been so mean, never so unkind
The times has never been so strained, worn so thin and fine
The life we knew is over now; there is no going back
The bottom's never been so low – my eyes are looking up

This is Me

This is me requesting permission to spread my wings and fly
This is me rejecting the notion we only live to die

This is me reaching out to you in hopes you'll take my hand
This is me hoping that you'll take me to the promised land
This is me believing in something that goes against all reason
This is me extending my faith in all that comes from you

This is not the end
This is not the last you'll see of me
This is only the beginning
This is everything I thought it would be

This is me trusting in what I cannot see
This is me throwing caution to the wind, scattering seeds
This is me giving up all control I used to think I had
This is me accepting what I cannot deny is true

Waiting For Me

Forever is a long time to make a promise to you
I can't see past my own shadow

I can't live past my own shoes

Today I'll be here waiting for my chance to live
I can't take care of tomorrow
When I'm still wrapped up in today

I don't know where I'll be tomorrow or where this dream will take me
I don't know where I'm going today
Or when this dream will end

But can I trust that you will be there when I get there
I want you to be the first one
That I see waiting for me

Someday I will be the person that the world wants me to be
Until then I can't promise anything
But I'm living for this dream

One look in your eyes tells me everything I need to know
You know me more than I know myself
I wanted you to see

I will never let you down, but I can never see what's coming
I will promise to be there
Even when I don't know where I am

I can't always be there, but God knows that I still try
The good life is still so far away
But I can see it in the distance

Open your eyes, focus and you can see it, too
I don't know what to do when we get there
But I'll figure it out along the way

What We've Done

What moments of your lifetime shall I write about
What fragments from your past would you like the light shined on
What seconds from your history would you like to have still framed
What minute would you like to have back to live again

I don't know if we can go back and undo what we've done
I don't know if it's all for the better or the worse
But I do know that life goes on, the battle is already won

It's such a noble thought to want to do it all over again
It's such a pleasant thought to think it's just that easy
It's such a sweet belief that one could simply slow down
It's such a beautiful image to take the best and leave the worst

Would you ever want to face the old days all over again
Would you ever want to face those demons you have left behind
Would you ever want to come back home once you've moved away
Knowing nothing will ever be the same

Dumb Dumb

Here comes dumb dumb, strolling down the street again
Pale face, blank look on his sad demeanor
He can't understand a shred of normal thinking
Tripping over cracks in the sidewalk

Strung out on some heavyweight indecision
Can't make up his mind about where he's living
In the real world or his imagination
Too bad, because he's missing on so much

Dumb dumb, here comes dumb dumb
Thumb thumb, he's living under something's thumb
Numb numb, he can't feel a single thing in the world
Scum scum, he gave up his morals to become it

Here comes dumb dumb, strolling down the street again
Pale face, blank look on her sad demeanor
She can't understand a shred of normal thinking
Tripping over cracks in the sidewalk

Strung out on some heavyweight indecision
Can't make up her mind about where she's living
In the real world or her imagination
Too bad, because she's missing on so much

Dumb dumb, here comes dumb dumb
Thumb thumb, she's living under something's thumb
Numb numb, she can't feel a single thing in the world
Scum scum, she gave up her morals to become it

March Of The Militants

They're on the march with their small minds and even smaller hearts
Hating everything that doesn't look like them
They've got it on the brain that everyone is out to kill them
They've lost their minds or gone insane

This is the march of the militants
This is hatred on parade
This is the march of the militants
This is their real life violent charade

No matter what you say or do they'll find a fault that's true
It rings inside their heads like gongs and bells that never seem to stop
Till they've exterminated the entire world all around them
They're out to pave their way to hell

They're on the march with their small minds and even smaller hearts
Hating everything that doesn't believe like them

Who Knows

You like to say you know it all, is it worth even saying
Do you know what it's like to be me, to walk on the edge of believing
You like to tell me every detail, is it worth recounting
All the holes in your stories are letting too much air into the pages

Who knows when the world will explode, when the bombs will be released from the silos
Who knows when the earth is going to shake rill it just can't shake anymore

You like to be the big man on the block, burning all the anthills
Just wait till the end of the line when you're the one on top
Meanwhile, I'll be standing below you running for cover
While you feel all the blues of the flame I'll be safe in the shade

Puppet Strings

They're pulling me on puppet strings, though I do not know their names
The faces all roll into one, it always feels the same
Against the grain, all better judgment, all better judgment in my heart
To fall into that trap, again, I'd surely fall apart

The same old faces in the crowd, circling the same old rounds
Nothing ever happens in this place, full of the same old sounds
Something has to change or break the mold they cast and gave a face
To simply fill the hole this isn't working anymore

I've come to find there's so much more, if only to even up the score
History won't change itself; life worth living quietly drowns out the roar
Throw away all of the chains that only serve to bind and freeze-frame time
Move on and make a brand new name, we can't burn out until we fly into the sun

What Was Formerly Known As

What was formerly known as the new kingdom fell
All of society's order went to hell
Not even the clairvoyants knew what was next
All their crystal balls fell into one hot mess

What was formerly known as the next in line
All of its new faces and mouths saw the signs
Not even the analysts knew what to expect
Their charts and graphs didn't give room for wrecks

Good riddance to the old days
Let them die is pastures gone and grey
I'm looking forward towards the future
Where all my coming days will be paid

Good riddance to the old guard
Their time has come they just haven't left
I'm looking forward towards a time
When businessmen in suits don't rule the world

Now faced with the rubble, the bricks, and the stones
No one has a word or a spare thought to throw

All of the businessmen have fled for the hills
The talking heads have abandoned their thrones

Revenge Of The Space Kid

They never should have counted him out; he made his way off the sidewalk
He kept his head in the clouds and he kept his feet down on the ground
To say he was a late bloomer may have been the understatement of the year
But when you're in this deep there's really nowhere else to go

The space kid took the reigns, sailed away to come back some day
His grand return was hailed high and hailed low
The space kid took on all the world and never lost his sight
You may not know it, but he knows more than you'll ever know

They never should have put him down or out; they didn't know just what they had
His was a spirit that would never return again; sometimes they never come back
To say he lost his way is putting it too easy, for some, yet others turn and run
Tell the story of his grand return to see the world acknowledge him for once

The Alien That Lives With You

I've seen the alien that lives with you
He is not me; he is not true
I've seen the look behind its eyes
It is not truth; it's only lies
I've read all about him circa 1984
Big brother is his alter; his ego is his form
I've heard its words, its work's comprise
Nothing but a pack of fine-printed lies

Its tentacles have made their way
Into every fiber of your being
And you don't see it
He's slowly draining you of lifeblood
And all the while he'll smile
And say it's all right, but soon enough
Slowly and suddenly quicker
You feel yourself circling the drain more often

I've seen his moves behind your back

He's like a salesman with a knack
I've seen him buy himself a favor here and there
In return he'll burn the love you gave him unaware
I've read about him circa 1969
He'll make you fight the battles he's tied himself into
I've heard its words; it's not the clearest form of thought
In fact it's rather nothing but an endless trail of knots

I've see the alien that lives in your midst
He can't be shown trust; his values went bust
I've seen the world through his eyes so long ago
It's one so far from love, too low to fit above
I've seen the ends circa 2004
When money wins the game and truth is put to shame
I've stood a distance and watched his pieces play
Chess with all those lives, naïve to darker days

Why Is It So Hard To Love A Tattooed Man

Why is it so hard to love a tattooed man
When the lions don't bite and the dragons aren't real
What is it about him that scares you so much
The scary faces aren't real and the flames aren't quite

Who are you to judge what is on the outside
With his back to the demons and his eyes on the light
Where are all your armies of the pure and the sane
What's a joker ever done when tears, like blood, fell like rain

Why is it so hard to love a tattoed man
When the drippings on his sleeves are his heart in his hands
What it is about the man that fears no needle
The ink on his skin will only wither and fade

Who are you to tell him what story he can tell
You haven't lived a day in his life
Where are all the freaks that stood outside in the lines
Waiting to be with him, to be by his side

Why is it so hard to catch the eyes of a man
Who wears his heroes and villains in the palms of his hands

When did it become so hard to read past his form
To see past the lines into his library mind

What I Need

You know what I need
A stronger heart and a spirit that's free
You know what I am
A soul in need of a helping hand

You know where I've been
To places I can never go back, again
You know what I've seen
Enough to know that there is more within me

Through the dark, walking blind
When I've lost my way
Through the lies and disguises
That only got in the way

To getting to you

You know what I need
A brand new start, a slate that's clean
You know what I am
A better man than when I started

You know where I'm going
Though the path I chose slowed me
You know what I'm seeking
A place to call home where you're leading me

Lilies

I don't know where you came from, but I hope that this is real
I can't help, but to want your time, it's just the way I feel
I want you to be near me – I so want you around
I pray I'm seeing clearly, so I don't miss the sweetest thing

In this world that I've found
In this world of all I've found

I feel like I just know you and that you know me too
I can't help, but to think you see – it's what I must believe is true
It's just too real to put aside, too real to put out of mind
I couldn't if I wanted to, so I hope that you will someday be

In my world taking up my time
In my world, the best thing in my life

I'm not a teenage dreamer, but you make me feel like one
I'm much too wise to fall too hard, but you make me feel that dumb
I'm not a love-struck romantic fool, but you make me sound the part
I'm no sucker to bring lilies to your house, unless it comes right from the heart

Is it true there is a lily in the field for everyone
Are you the one out there for me – if I'm not careful could I lose you

Look To The Monitor

In the midst of this confusing scene
Who are you and what are all of these
Little statues that we used to call man
Little angels that we used to call womankind

In the latter part the war was won
But the cost had very well undone
What it was we were fighting for
The truth we realized was kicked out the door

Look to the monitor – look for a sign
If it's going to come the source will be divine
Look to the monitor, look to the sky
When the rain comes it's going to rain down fire

Lizards here among us speak in forked tongue words
Prophets speak so vague we hardly concern
Ourselves with anything they say to be our cause
In the end it's just a game you can't pause

Nothing In Our Hands

Till all is well, as it should be, we will be on this road
Till the demons turning wheels are banished from our souls
Till the sun rises high on our desires
Till the sun goes down and rests upon your holy fires

Till time stops slipping through our hands, sand in the hourglass
Till our demands and stands are less for show and more for keeps
Till we stop coming here to be entertained in vain
Till our ambitions stop circling the drain

Until that time we will be waiting
For something coming we can never ever plan
Until that time we will be pacing
Drawing lines and walking miles where we stand

When all is said and done, everything in its place
Even the stars, even the sun
When everything is in its place and our eyes are opened
We will understand

Until that time we will be waiting
For something coming we can never ever plan
Won't be it funny when we find out
This was all for nothing, nothing in our hands

Useless Soundscape

It's such a useless soundscape
You might as well turn off the politics already
The only life worth living is the examined life
And if there's one thing we all know is unexamined
For the most part, it's politics

In an arena where truth is one percent
Of everything said and done, what's the point
It doesn't seem to make sense to me
When one tells me it's my civic duty
To pick the least of two poisons when I don't want either one

It's all so futile it's almost laughable
It's all so laughable it's almost excessively selfish

Good time at another's expense
Funny, the term "at another's expense"
That's almost the definition of life, isn't it

It's all lived at another's expense
No matter how small of a living we try to eek out
No matter how humble one tries to live
No matter how simple, no matter how invisible

We all leave a trail behind
We all take a toll at another's expense
I can't help but think the only life worth living
Is an examined life where we are the least expensive
At another's expense

Then, again, it could be as Morrison said
Roughly, what you say doesn't have to make sense
As long as it impacts somebody in a personal, emotional way
Either way, I've found politics does none of that
And is truly a useless soundscape

All The World's Laugh Track

I've seen you live your life to the laugh track
The flashing pictures and colors on screen
Does it really tell you what you need to hear
And show you what you need to see

I've seen you waste your days staring blankly
Off into the cold, void distance
Unblinking eyes, unthinking minds
They tell a story, so sad and predestined

I've seen the lives they live in their false world
They're always smiles and jokes and nods
It paints a picture that's so wrong for me
To ever believe to be true

I've seen the minds floating down the gutters
Down the drains and into the pipes
Every time another one hits the sewer line

An angel loses wings

Live your life to the laugh track
Never bother to try to swing back
Die in bliss with a dumb smile
On your face, walking the sad mile

I've seen a life go wasted too peacefully
We we're never meant to go out that way
We're floating ducks in a carnival game from hell
It must be bliss to think you're doing so well

Live your life to their time code
Sync your beats and ticks to the drone
Take in the words of the sad machines
Pulling your plug, plucking your angel wings

<u>Days On The Radio</u>

I'd rather spend my days on the radio
Singing to someone whose name I'll never know
I'd rather spend my days as headless voice
Preaching the gospel of my heart and soul

I'd rather be with you in obscurity
Next to transistors with no heart or soul
Only pumping the messages put in them
As long the sources are truthful

Days on the radio
Days in my own head
Days spent in paradise
Till a storm sweeps in

I'd rather spend my years in a broken place
That's closer to home than anywhere else
I'd rather avoid all of your purity
Your purity's a lie that you've bought hook and line

I'd rather dine in the halls of the rejects
Than with all the princes and kings and queens

I'd rather have the dignitaries see my back
My face would rather be seen by those who love me

Days breaking down again
Days learning lessons, all over and then
Days breaking stride again
To clean up the pieces of me on the floor

Your Daily Brainworm

I don't need to hear this, all you talking heads
Take your bright ideas and put them to bed
I don't need to feel this sadness and pain
Knowing decisions you make will bring this world shame

We don't need another person tracking mud in the halls
Slinging dirt and throwing arrows, closing in walls
We don't need another liar at the wheel of this steed
Another false messiah we'll be knee deep in creeds

It's digging, boring into my brain
I can't run – it's everywhere, like earth and rain
It's sucking, draining me of life and strength
This blind machine, so sad, so lost, and full of rage

We don't need any apes on the shoulders of men
Get the ticks in your brain removed from your head
We don't need all your tangled words everywhere
Teach the voices that talk all at once how to share

Maybe then we'll stand a chance in this race
Maybe then we'll walk at a less reckless pace
Maybe then we'll see what's been in front of us all along
Maybe then we'll hear the chatter from the back of the bus

Even The Devil's Caught Reading The Bible

I'd never throw you under the bus
So why is my chest being crushed by a tire
I'd never drag your name in the mud
Why does its utterance set people on fire

I'd never give you up to the reds
So why am I here on Joe's trial
I'd never break our promise of faith
Why did you give me back my ring

Once in a while, I'm sure
Even the devil's caught reading the Bible
I've seen it enough to believe
Even your morals have gone out of style

The Art Gallery Waiting Room

I'm waiting for something
I'm waiting for something to happen
I'm waiting for you
I'm waiting for you to blow my mind

I've stared at the walls
I've stared at the walls for hours
I've stared at the posers
I've stared at the posers holding their breath

You're here in spirit
You're here in spirit, words, and sound
You're here in the details
You're here in the details no one's found

You've laid all the tracks straight
You've laid all the tracks straight, through to the end
You've set all the switches
You've set all the switches to turn on you

There's no writing on the walls
There's no echo from the halls
There are no breadcrumbs for a trail
There's no reason to chase our tails

Basement Jazz

Consider this the voices from the basement

Consider this the voices of the others
Consider this the rain that's in your gutters
Consider this the rain that you never saw coming

Remember this like ghosts in the moonlight
Remember this in your shadows and in your dreams
Remember this as stuck in your conscience
Remember this in canvas and in portrait

All the players have gone downstairs
All the players both foul and fair
All the players have picked up their instruments
Ready to play for eternity

All the players have their caps topped
With a feather in their brims
All the players are wearing grins
As wide as the devil's when he's won

This is basement jazz
This is the sound of your subconscious
These are the devils that want out
These are the angels that dance with those devils

This is the music that plays
This is the music that lulls you off to sleep
This is what you hear when you don't want to sleep
This is what keeps you up all night wondering

Consider these your final chances to join them
Consider these your last offers to lay it down

Sweeperman

Back and forth, forth and back
Stealing his way through this strange land
Time and time, again and again
Finding his way to the same stance

Same bad time, same bad place
Names may change, but people stay the same

Always the same, always different
The hands on the clock spin – they're in on the game

The dust always settles and gets moved around
Just to be put back in its place
Try as we might, we can't move the chains
You can't damn up the same river twice in your life

The man goes back, the man goes forth
Making a new mess as we clean up the last
We try our best, though effort is nice
It's all grains of sand, hours in a glass

The Imperative

There's a moral to this story, but I don't what it is
There's a reason for this madness, but I can't see through the fizz
There's a want for every need, but I don't know what I have
There's a time for every crash, but I can't time up the wreck

There's a laugh for every tear, but I don't know what was said
There's a smile for every season, but I can't read your lips
There's a dog for every day, but I'm still stuck in this cage
There's a random act of kindness, but not this day in age

This is the imperative; this is the reason we all live
This is the imperative; this is the reason we all breathe
This is the imperative; this is the reason we all cringe
This is the imperative; this is the reason we're unhinged

There's an inch for every foot, but I don't know where to hold
There's a mend for every break, but I still can't find the stitch
There's an echo for the voice, but I don't know what to say
There's a man inside the box, but I put the nails in

Tortoise Colored Glasses

The sketchy character with pads of notes and memorizations rote
The loose lips seem to glean most anything most unserene
The crowds of ups and downs and towns have made their rounds and sounds
The meanings all were lost when fire drove the monsters out

So it goes the poet wrote as he went on to say
Tomorrow may not be much better than it was today

The people in their herds moving left and right
Putting up fences splitting day from night
Breaking into groups and genres so small they're unseen
It doesn't make much sense to you and it doesn't to me

The nonchalant with deadpan tongues speaking words that seem unsung
The books of hymns and rhymes of his and hers are out of time
The numbers in the dance, they put us in an end-times trance
The focus comes and goes till we're unseated by our pants

The lines that stretch around the building don't know what they're there to see
The spectacle itself is now the show-stealing scene
The rants and raves and misbehaving minds and tongues don't cease
The bar is lowered every word they speak and bone that creaks

<u>7464746474647484</u>

I'm living to an irregular rhythm
My heart can't keep up with you
I'm walking at a pace most random
My steps don't match up with my blues

I'm seeing in stereo and hearing in mono
My system must have blown a fuse
I fear I've become no longer useful
My time has come to go into recluse

I'm tearing down a track that's running out
My legs can't turn on the breaks
I'm burning out fast, dying young
My legacy's turned into cliché

I'm murdering the image I made
My destruction done the proper way
I'm turning the world on its head
My view of eternity is better this way

I'm tearing it down all around me
One brick and mode at a time
I'm throwing the game for the final time
In a matter of minutes and rhyme

I'm writing the lines for my final words
In meter and epitaph and sign
I'm leaving a trail of my life's work
In the tracks of my paths all behind

Fields Of Plastic Roses

I'm walking in a field of roses
Not a single one appears to be real
Everyday becomes a sea of people
Not a single one appears to be true

As the night comes on my hopes are weakened
By what I see around me and makes me cry
As the hours passing by keep drifting
I'm sailing into dreams away from this place

Float away, float away
To much better places and times
Drift away, drift away
To more peaceful states of mind

Come back some day, come back some day
When things have changed for the better
Make time to pray, make time to pray
That better days are coming

Enough times around this same track
It makes me see things for what they are
Enough times left wanting more than this
It makes me dream I could just disappear

Kings, Queens, And Pawns

I've seen castle walls crash down in piles at your feet
I've seen ants come forth in droves driving out monsters and beasts

I've seen the sky turn red and bleed sweet crimson shooting stars
I've seen the natural world revolt – in blindness I see through your eyes

We've seen the masses cry out loud for something more than we've been sold
We've seen buildings scrape the sky trying to reach the gods we mold
We've broken down and built back up these simple things we call our lives
We've lost it all and gained the world when we went blind and learned to see

Still I've never seen a soul so deep as yours
I've never felt a love so deep and pure
Still I've never held a moment like this in my hands
I believe I never will like yours, again

The greatest kingdoms all will fall to dust back down to earth
Kings and queens and all their pawns lose everything in the end

It's For The Best

You used to fly so high like paper cranes up in the sky
But then they shot you down like pigeons made of clay
You used to smile so free for me and everyone who passed your way
Now there's nothing left to smile for they've gone and clipped your wings

It doesn't have be so dark at the rainbow's end
It doesn't have to feel so heavy to hold your head up high

Where did all the blue sky go
Why do all the flower children cry
What have all the dreamers turned into
I'd have to say it's for the best

We used to be so good together, all the puzzle pieces fit
But now the world stepped in and divided us all
We used to share a moment all in fun, never thinking of the pay
Now the only way to stay alive is to bribe us all the way

We don't have to be so tired at the end of the day
We don't have to be so sick of making sense of everything

Say It Again

I'm picking out daisies that I think would work for you
I think you'd look nice if you let your hair down, too
I threw away my pride to write this down for you
I hope it reaches you sometime soon before I lose it

Say it again, say it again
Say it out loud to me this time
Say it with heart, say it with soul
To let me know you mean it

I'm making my mind up and I think that you're just fine
I'm putting it all out this time to let you realize
I'm wearing my heart on my sleeve, maybe you haven't seen
I'm dropping my armor for this one last final scene

Maybe it wasn't meant to be
Maybe only time will tell
Maybe I'm just making a fool of myself
Oh, what the hell…what the hell

Songs That Sing

I don't know what's going on, anymore, I must be strong
Can you see this heart of mine, set so free I'd lose my mind
Everyone has got to let it go, all this trouble, don't you know
Everybody needs a little peace; somewhere the air is light and free

Deep inside you see it too, it's in your eyes so crystal blue
Oceans deep, it's so serene, it's too bad we've lost that scene
Take some time to breathe, to see exactly what it means
To be the real thing and hear the songs that sing

Star Seas And Trails

Come back to the world, daydreamer
Even though things down here aren't much clearer
Come back down to Earth, stargazer
Even though everything is so much deeper

Do you know where you are
Is this a dream

Do you know what you are
A king or a queen

Return to the clouds, my angel
This world isn't ready for you, right now
Return to the scene you came from
This place isn't safe for those like us

Do you know what's going on
There's so much more to come
Do you know why this happens
Even to the best of us

Are you swimming the seas of the stars
Do the beaches seem so far away
Are you leaving a trail to follow
Do you know the way to get back home

Come down once again, all is quiet.
Return to the world that needs you now
Come down from the clouds, we're waiting
For your words and your ways to save us somehow

Stealing From My Dreams

I'd like to show you what it's like to spin
Out of control and enjoy it
I'd like to take you for a mile in my shoes
And report it to the world

I'd like to see you in my arms
As we hover above the Earth, so carefree
I'd like to see you in my dreams
As regular phantasms I could see

I can see this being for real
I can see you stealing from my dreams
Can you see yourself in my mind
Flying so high up in space like a queen

I'd like to see you as an angel

Only reporting to me, but not to control you
I'd wish to be in your company forever
You're the only one who really knows me

I'd like to be so far from here, from anything
Anything that reminds me of something other than you
I'd like to feel what it's like to be floating in the clouds
Only holding your hand, like a daydream

I'll find the door to this reality
I'll turn the handle till I twist it off
I'll find a way out of this blissful hell
And take you with me all the way

This Tiger's Tale

This tiger's full of tales, each word is filled with nails
The road is never ending – is this what we have to look forward to
With every sentence spoken, free minds, they fill the jails
Then, keys get tossed away, what are we supposed to do

For every pendulum swing the men in black robes bring
Another box to shut away a dreamer's schemes to play
One more for glory's pride, our fame kept all inside
Or else we just spin our tires pleasing all the fools

Is this all there is here for a while let's move on, let it be said
There's nothing said worth keeping now, nothing worthy of being read

You Look Good On The Radio

You like the idea of me, but the real thing sends you running
You were always so close at night, by day the distance just kept coming
You seemed so sure of things, but you let the past rush back in
You couldn't keep a straight head if you tried; you spent too much time in it

You're always on the fence it seems and can't commit to anything
Your mind rides the razor's edge, while your tongue cuts me into ribbons
I tried to help you settle down, but your doors were too wide open
I tried to give you something to reach for; the hangers-on were all that was spoken

You spread your love too wide; the damn door was always open
You never kept it locked, not once for me, you let the past roll in like thunder
You let a crack turn into a fault line and always pushed me in it
You tried to take me on a ride, but eventually the yo-yo stops spinning

I've seen you play the victim game, but I don't believe a single line of it
Though I may still be a bit naïve my mind is sharp and ears are open
I've given all I can to you because you can't strip down the broken
I've learned a little something from you – never trust a hand of cards not spoken

<u>Yesterdays And Nevers</u>

I'm borrowing some hope from you
Maybe you can tell me if it's real
This is all I've got to say
Something that I can't believe myself

Denial has a strong backhand
It hits just as hard the second time
Where you are and where I am
How did it ever get so far

Nothing is for real when you think about it
Nothing is for shame when you read about it
No one is to blame when you preach about it
No one can explain when we talk about it

I'm living for my yesterdays
Every other day has gone
We can't change the future
We can only rewrite the past

Victors write the books we read
Losers, we all fall apart
All we have is what we make
Make it something that will last

Never lose that smile you feel
Never give up the lips you've sealed
Never write those letters that never end
Never break, until you get the chance to bend

Mina Birds On The Cable Cords

Mina bird in the courtyard's been feeling blue since the day that you left
The knights have shed their armor and let the sun fill in for the stars
The broken picture frames and mirrors have repaired themselves in honor of you
The blackest clouds in the sky turned purple the day they thought they could try

It's so sad to see you go
To think of what you left behind
It's so sad to see you go
Where to send all the letters you wrote

The rosy pink of the flowers and children has withered since the day that you left
The workers building the streets they named after you have let them decay
The words the poets wrote to welcome you home quit their post when you made your mistake
The wind that blew the banners high in the sky for your name settled down in your leave

As The Snakes Begin To Coil

Onward soldiers march into desert sands
Concrete jungles stand over our heads grand
Grand stands full of sheep cheer for what they reap
What they fear to sow goes all but unknown

Backwards culture moves, people's faith shows true
Leaving those behind, those who are not youth
For our words we speak we know nothing new
All our mouths can preach are our own self-truths

The theatre curtain rises as we start another day
The mob is staring at the backdrop we create
The mood intensifies as the crowd begins to boil
With thoughts, and words, and motions the snakes begin to coil

Braggadocios swag, they've got it in the bag
Their places are all set, no room for safety nets
All the big wigs pine, for their own grandeur shines
More true in their own eyes than the people they despise

Snakes, like mice and men, have a their stake in the end
We all play our part; the final scene is around the bend
We've been building up to this crescendo
Round and round we spin, where we'll go who knows

Tigers And Tails

A tiger's full of tails, a road that's strewn with nails
Is this all that we have got to look forward to
When every word brings a sentence and all the jails are full
Tell me just what are we supposed to do

For every pendulum swing the death dealers bring
It's just another reason to trail off into nothing
One for the glory and shame, the price of everyone's fame
Is a ride on down the spiral and into the tank

If this is all there is, then what's left to be said
If this is all that's left, then what's worth being kept

Nervous men with projector screens in place of eyes gaze like beams
Drowning you of life and strength, only quickening your wake

Souls And Signs

So they go, the roads they know, the places I should never go
So they blow, the winds they show, the way that I must follow

I relinquish my soul to the universe's shoulders

So they're told, the stories old, the young hearts so unaware of time
So they're sold, the moments we live, minutes bought and fed to the lions

Take this all away and let me see what is real
Remove the blinders from my eyes; show me what no one can steal

Strip it down to souls and signs so I can feel between the lines
Rebuild my heart to let you in, to let the new world be my home

So our lives go on and on, the years they pass like setting suns
So our memories, like the sand, the glass they're trapped in breaks in our hands

I can forget and leave it behind, step into the chapters that are opening in due time

The Soldier's Revolution Around The Sun

Are we the center of the universe
Or a passing plane in the night
Are we the one everyone's come to see
Or a temporary flavor caught in their sights

We see the world through lens and microscope
Picking it apart before we ever get to know
What's really there, is it worth slowing down to see
Just forget it and drop a bomb on the whole damn scene

Are we a force worth throwing our weight around
Or another one antagonizing way too loud
Are we the chosen ones to tell everyone what to do
Or a megalomaniac with something to prove

The soldier's revolution around the sun
Another state is claimed so the day is done
Are we to blame for the hatred we bring on ourselves
Is it so wrong to see the truth, the light, who would tell

Are we unfaithful if we challenge the powers that be
Or a patriot much taller than all else can see
Are we abandoning our call if we step aside
Or a thinking man who's tired of taking the ride

Codenames And Bliss

I'm tired of the same old thing
The broken records and broken strings
The worn out lines and pages of empty words
Are a thing of the past, tell me, have you heard

I'm wearing skins of the new animal within me
The ties are cut with the past that wouldn't let me free
The shift has changed – a new tide is coming
Are these the words of a madman or is it me

Everything is not what it used to be
Everything's changed around
The furniture's not where it used to sit
The feeling is gone from the sound

The places I used to know have disappeared
And filled up with codenames and bliss
The reasons for carrying on have changed
For all the wrong reasons and this

The puppet strings are gone – my hands are free
To feel a brand new pulse running in my blood
To run the gauntlet, hit me with everything you've got
My time is short, but lasts longer than what you've bought

My tastes have changed and so have my enemies
I'm finding out all the hard ways around this world
I'm losing parts every single step that I take
It's well and good, I'm shaking the rust off of me

I'm standing up at the end of the final round
The final bell didn't herald my swan song call
The first of you who is perfect may cast a stone
As for the rest can you just leave my kind alone

<u>You Today</u>

Your today is a bad dream
You're on the left side of the right scene
Your tomorrow doesn't look so good
Not even in the right light

Sadly, it's all over
All has been said and done
Madly you chase your tail
Until there's nowhere else to run

Your last trip was a fall down
You're on the bottom of the chain now
You're hanging on by a loose thread

Another rip in the line you'll lose your grip

You're on the losing end of this line
Fearing the worst will come in quick time
Watching as life passes you by
Buying the life you sold to get high

There For You

Dreamers with tears in your eyes, I'm there for you
Lovers with no hearts left inside, I'm there for you
Poets with no more strength for your words, I'm there for you
Children with no more youth in your soul, I'm there for you

Fighters with no strength to go on, I'm there for you
Survivors with no rope to hold on, I'm there for you
Mothers with no time in the day,I'm there for your
Father's in the skids with no breaks, I'm there for you

When the world beats you down and you feel thrown away
When you can't carry on, there's no more game to play

The Mob

Here comes the mob, they're back again, for a little more action
As if they didn't get enough the last time
A demonstration of their simple minds

Here come the talking heads with little more than empty words
As if they didn't fill your head up last time
Showing us where their hot air ends up

They are so fickle they don't know what to do
They can't make up their minds or tell me what is true
They are so in a hurry all the time, it seems
They can't be trusted to hold onto their own dreams

Here comes the crowd, again, calling for some more
What more is there to give them
We've given them our souls

Here come the puppets, their strings are showing
They dance and move as they are told
By hands that have no face to hold

Sweet Songs About Nothing

I want to send a message to you to let you know our time is through
Things change and people move on, we can't keep singing the same old song
You won't believe where I have gone or how the stars have hidden my sun
But I don't think you want to know, in your own world this isn't so

Sweet songs about nothing are my favorite things in the world
That's why I wrote this song for you

I saw you just the other day and you seemed just the same
You're jackets and pins define you, your drinks and attitudes wind you
Into a tizzy that's all so familiar it's almost second nature
To not feel anything at all, isn't that true, stranger

Sweet songs about no one are the saddest things in the world
But still we dance and sing along

Rot In Here

Paddling out into the sea there's no one else here, but me
Leaving all of you behind, no second thoughts or clocks to wind
All of you can live your lives on the same sad train to die
In a sad state of affairs and mind, the same you've come to define

Flying off out into space to leave your face behind
All the scars you're subject to were of your own design

All of you can keep your lies, saving face while killing time
In a place where no one minds if you're not interesting or refined
I've made my mind up this time; I'm not going to rot in here with you
I've made amends with everyone and everything I care to do

You've set your own course for mediocrity and bliss
Blind and senseless to everything but yourself, swearing that you still exist

I Erased Myself From History

I erased myself from history
Just pretend that I was lost and never found
I left behind all of your misery
Go on and tell the world what you believe is fair

Distance, time, and life cure it all
Except the pale, dumb, and blind
Time heals all wounds except the deepest ones
The self-inflicted come to mind

I'll pull the veil down for necessity
Exposing the holes and propped up molds
To let the world see their reality
To separate what's gold from all the fools

I jumped the rails of your runaway train
Bound for nowhere, fast and way too late
I'd rather walk for miles free of shame
Go on and ride till you can't recognize your face

I'll do the same thing tomorrow
The very trick I did today and the day before
The great escape act of the century
It's what you do and not what you see or say

I erased myself from history
The photo albums, journals, and minds
I left behind all of your misery
For a sweeter, softer kind of sound and sign

Hell Is Other People

When only God knows why only devils are awake at this hour
When dogs know not to bite they just can't help themselves
We're all in chains; we convince ourselves we're free
Hell is the world that you make all around you – hell is other people

When even angels know to stay right where they are
When it's clear they've lost their footing and their hold on us
We're all in this together, scratching, clawing, biting wraiths

Hell is the world we've made, indeed – hell is other people

You never get what you want this way, but you'll get what you need, just pray
The dream is a lie, so it seems invariably
Vision is a scheme, stereotypically, and topically
It's always brightest before the dawn and then it all comes down along

Side with the pretty one and sweet tongues
See how long it takes to lose faith, one by one
How many times does this have to happen before you learn what is real
It's not in postcards and films spun on steel; coils and bolts are simply tools to conceal

Failure To Take Off

My head is stuck up here in the clouds
I'm flying in circles and I just can't land
I've got a white-knuckle grip on dreams
And things that only slip through my hands

Outrunning the black clouds that follow me
Is hard to do with your feet off the ground
I'm not trying to be a bad trip for you
I'm just trying to rocket off towards the sound

Failure to take off, no bother to get prepared to land
Failure to break off all the loose appendages in my hands

Bottle rockets soar up into the sky
My engines won't click on for their life
Fireworks and dragons flies aren't shy
I can't get myself to ask why life's unkind

The silver lining I figure is this
My feet weren't laid with the wet cement
I may be a space kid all the time
It's better than playing the part of the mimic or the swine

Vultures For Fate

The boy exploded, his soul imploded
You laughed at him then, now, you're crying bleeds thin

Tears, hollow, held together with pins

His life was worthless as far as your sight believes
Your words were loaded
He didn't see it coming

I know the reason; it's not the seasons
It's all the treasons and they're still breeding
And seeding creation

You know what I feel; you know what I'll steal
Only the good the stuff
The ones that you love

The exploding boy, what a great big mess
Who's left to clean him up, now, who can stand to read the transcript
Who can stand to see the wreck

It's way too little, a little too late
You're all just vultures, now
Vultures for credos and fate

How do you feel knowing what you know
How do you sleep knowing what you did
Spinning webs with iron stints

You know that you killed him with all of your grins
Behind his back is where it started
That's where it always begins

Into Her Little World

She will give you the world, and then she'll take it all away
It's nothing to her, nothing more than a game she plays
Still I come back for more, knowing just what I'll get
I'm hoping maybe this time she'll let me in

Into her little world, her snow falling crystal ball
Into her little world, the four walls she built up around her

Though I'm not sure what she's made of, it's nothing you can see with your eyes

It's something so much more mysterious, like a gem, or a deserted, hunted, haunted prize
You can spend your whole life searching, but you will never crack her
It s something deeper, it's a sign, you have to catch or you've lost her

Time Stood Still

Wherever the wind blows me is where I find my soul
Whenever your eyes hold me is when I lose my tongue
Wherever the seasons take me is where I find my heart
Whenever your words shake me is when I lose my feet

I'll hold my heart in my hands, for you I'd show the world
What's in my dreams, across the sands, as time and our lives unfold

Wherever these days throw me is where I must end up
Whenever your memories remind me is when I leave reality
Wherever the scene is changing is when I reach for you
Whenever your face awakens me is when I'm flying high

I'll wear your grace as a robe, for you I'd lay down the world
What's in your eyes is a pearl, a single, stolen moment on hold

Wherever these daydreams find me is where I leave my shoes
Whenever you bring me back is when I know I'm not alone

Time I wish would stand still

Chasing The Wind

I left by the road less traveled, the one that was meant for me
The back roads hit the hardest, the best shots, they set you free
I started in one direction and never turned back
I've left some behind, abandoned; they'll come to learn it was for the best

You're chasing the wind, chasing your tail
Where this all leads we both know, but you fail
To simply move on and let it die
Let its time come to pass like the night

You knew what was happening from the start
You knew it was coming, but hardened your heart

Your reached for the sky as it withered away
Crawling in the trenches where your body will stay

I tried to pretend there was something to be salvaged from the wreck that was
I tried to pretend we were winning the battle that could not be won
I tried to pull you from the fire – you just would not budge
You made up your mind to expire, taking hammers to walls made of mud

Something had to change; I knew it would not be you
So I took my chances with my dignity and the truth
I'm sure that they all meant well, but it didn't work out that way
Don't look for me when the bottom drops out, I won't be around

When the world falls in around you, you can't refuse to move
It's going to break and it's breaking down, don't tell me that you can't see
When all the faces fade you close your eyes
Seeing the world for what it really is, it makes you want to cry

Shake the dirt from your feet
Shake the dust from your shoes
Pick up the pieces left
Hit the road with nothing to hide or lose

Nowhere To Be Seen

In a world that's moved on and love, it means nothing
Devotion is shallow and revolution is all that's on their minds
The old guard has passed away, the heroes all but disappeared
Now it's down to us three, taking on the world and its machines

In a time and place that's grown cold and full of bold ambition
Brotherhood is sparse, often sold, but deserves great recognition
The small and the few have taken up the cause
We know what the price is only to stand, no choice to fall

Can you see the future, look into your crystal ball
And if you see me coming let me know if it's a trap for us all
Can you see my next move, will you tell me what is soon to come
What becomes of my brothers, least of all myself, should I fall

I've found great love and lost it and the courage to lead the way

Allegiance lies in the farthest corners, everywhere else but home, become strayed

Where Have The Years Gone

Every baby's breath she takes is another declaration of her innocence
Every tiny step her feet make on her way toward young lady-ness
Every twinkle in her eye is another reason not to count her out
Every laugh or smile and moment passing by

Where have the years gone is what we will we be asking
Where has the time gone is what we seek to find

Every inch scratched into the doorway's frame is another notch in the passage of time
Every lock of hair on her sweet head is a reason to catch their eye

Years Of Wreckage

I stand against the world, a solitary man
It's how I came into this life and how I'll play my hand
What's coming for me I can see from a mile away
I'll put up my best fight and hold the rest in faith

Buried under years of wreckage
Falling off me day by day
I'm becoming something brand new
It's a miracle that only you do

There's so more to me than what your eyes can see
Deeper than oceans are layers the you're not reaching
Pieces of my past are scattered all over the place
If you can look past that you can see my true face

Long ago I would not have seen myself this far
Then again, those days were so bizarre
Nothing seemed to hold or keep it all together
Now, I'm living in the time that I call forever

No Words

No words fit the description of man whose hands are broken and soul is on his sleeve
No title fills the space in boxes and comfortable storage small minds try to conceive

Only this nondescript vague notion is the closest you can pin him down
Only this unclear presentation, the life lived and progeny spread around

He has no name, though we all know his face, no home, because he keeps on the move
He has no place that can tie him down to stay, no face that one can claim too soon

Only this blurb on a page, unknown to many out of sight and mind
Only this consideration and labor of love will remain in the books left behind

The Best I'll Give You

I know what you think you want, perfection and its charms
You think you'll be safe and warm in its arms
Understand one thing before you fall into its hands
It's simply all an act to hide the fear of life and chance

You know where you have been, where you have felt alone
Trusting all the pretty faces and all the lies they've sewn
Come to grips with just one thing – promise me you will
There's more beyond a smile behind the eyes, so still

You will find that you can see into their hearts for miles
The dirty tracks where pavement lacks, but loving all the while
To polished facades, shining reflections, cloudy in the dark
As light rains down above the crown the sky hides from us, unseen

The best I'll give you is all of my heart
The best I'll offer is all I can impart
I'll give you all the best, all that I have left
You will get the best of me until my dying breath

It can be hard to see who is real
It can wear so much on your soul
It can take so long to finally get there
Keep open eyes and a heart unfouled, still fair

Face To Face

I'm waiting for the sun to come, to invigorate my soul, again
I'm feeling the weight of my own skin dragging me down within

I've dropped my anchor here, though I'm not sure why or where this is
I was simply drawn to this place to meet my self again, face to face

Face to face with myself, the same old stare down begins
Face to face, this is my world, living out of the same suitcase, again

You're waiting for me to come around; your patience is much appreciated
You've watched me drag my chains; so long I can't understand or see through it
How you hold on to someone drowning, until they learn to swim, again
Till they come back home to stare down their old sins, face to face

House Of Cards

This is the house of cards stacked up
The wall built to keep us out
This is the stretch of faded desert walked down
The road opened up for you and no one else

These are the faces long ago rejected
The hands that tried to pick them up
These are the words not just spoken
These hearts have been broken too

Locked away inside ivory towers
Happier now in new bliss and fake smiles
Hide everything reflecting what you don't want seen
Know that I'll be waiting, but don't wait for me

Doors won't stay closed forever
Walls eventually come down
Whether or not we are inside
What is to happen pulls us aground

Never changing what we can't understand
It's hard to always be in demand
Even stones broken free from the road
At the end of the day find a new home

I'll Wait

Your eyes, they tell a story your mouth won't let you say

When words don't come that easily don't speak words that should be prayed
In stillness, silent reverence, I see you standing proud and great
When words don't have a chance to be stumbled upon or get in the way

I haven't met you yet, you don't even know who I am
Still, I'm bold enough to say to you that I can't wait

For one transgressing moment when my entire world crashes down
When walls come tumbling, tumbling down to the ground
I'll wait for you if you wait for me, if it means I have to lose it all
I'll wait to see if I have to start over, till doubt, likes birds of prey, pass over

Lost In A Dream

I'm looking into those eyes, though we're a million miles apart
I feel like I'm so far from home because that's exactly where I am
I don't recognize my face anymore, can you tell me, do you see what I see
I woke up feeling lost, still inside of a dream I just can't seem to wake up from

Lost and stuck in a dream or just some nightmare in disguise
I'm running on legs that feel so heavy, can you feel all the eyes on me, now

I'm in control of these limbs, every motion phoned in from miles away
I see a house on down the way and can't help but feel that's where I'm going
I see that you still live there, can you tell me, do I, as well
Before I had a chance to ask you I see you live there with somebody else

You will see my back as I move on again, that is if you stop to turn and look
Otherwise, you'll never even know I came by, even out of curiosity, only to wake up here

Running Title

It's a brand new level of intense
When they grey bleeds into the pink
It doesn't matter what you read or who you know
It's where you've been and what you think

All the time spent trying to get control
You're trying to wrangle something wrong
Every whisper in your ear is watered down
It's time to write the words to your own song

When you wake up the sun is shining bright
Step outside and it starts to rain
The titles all just blur into each other
The doldrums will fill you with pain

We're getting pulled into the atmosphere
Filling up the room and choking me down
We're getting pulled into the broken chair
I just don't have it in me to sit down

What's Your M.S., Partner

What's your M.S., partner, your deadline's come and gone
Still, you're waiting for the train to pick you up on the run
What's your M.S., partner, your plane has come and gone
Still, you're waiting for your ticket to fly, all you have to do is spread your wings

I think I know what's going on here, though you can't see a thing
It's something so much deeper, but you won't let me in

What's your M.S., partner, you threw the game and the works
Still, you want your paycheck to pull you through this week
What's your M.S., partner, your taxi's come to a stop
The driver put the breaks on hard, but you didn't thank him for his knocks

What's your M.S., partner, you've got your mind to make
What's your bright idea now, pay up the dealer or shake

The Hurricane's Eye

As I was sitting in the hurricane's eye
I watched and waited for the moment to pass by
It never came, but it never went
It's not a loss if none was spent
I find it hard to believe I could sit and stare
While the world around me stood naked, bare
For everyone to point and laugh
With eyes so blind and ears so deaf

As I was waiting in the corner of the church

I waited for the moment when it starts to hurt
It never came, but it never went
I couldn't lose if I didn't spend
If no one cried and no one lied where would we be now
In a cycle where the system's only slowing down
Stepping forward once, stepping back twice
You can dream your whole life; it must be nice

The story goes, it never ends as long as it is heard
Once we stop retelling history it's not a word
Repeat it over in a sentence that was fed to you
While you were telling me a lie you swore was true
I find it hard to believe you could sit and stare
At the world standing naked, bare
What would drive a man to point and laugh
When his eyes are blind and ears are deaf

I'll be preying in the corner of the church
Waiting for the moment when it starts to hurt
It hasn't come and it hasn't gone
I'm not to blame for what I haven't done
If no one died and no one lied where would we be now
In a cycle where the system's only slowing down
I'm stepping forward once and stepping back twice
You can dream your whole life; it must be nice

Picking Up Strays

You're picking up strays like a doormat; they're walking all over you just like you're flat
You give them a good house and home, in return for the deed they let you fall
Right onto your face, over and over, while they drain your blood and ride your back
It's a brand new thing, a twist on an old game until it hits them hard and all goes black

Don't you know that stray cats and people, they all leave the same mess
The only difference, far as I can tell is that animals feel regret
As for you, I'm not certain, there's not a single bone in your entire body bag
That stood by me when I was alone

I'm talking to all of the hangers on who don't even know it, but resemble a leach
Every day is a sick metamorphosis until the cycle is complete
Toiling and struggling to stay on board on the ride they thought was free

This time I'm the bearer of bad news, it's time you made tracks, I believe

Mister Fiend

Mister fiend, clumsy man in tweed
Chasing rabbits, half mad, half machine
On a horse, a carriage made of steam
Driven sane by sweat dropping in beads

Mister fiend's lease on life carved in stone
Never shaken, till this time left alone
Chasing shadows, pocket lights, from the dash
If only life looked half as good in the camera's flash

Mister train, running hard, fast, and loose
All the cars out for themselves, especially the caboose
Rocking left, flailing right, twisting on, losing sight
Headlights cracked from the madness, not the might

Mister vein, flowing free, through our misdeeds
Cleaning shop, clearing closets, with skeleton mops
Flotsam breadcrumbs, jetsam scraps for the rest
Ignore the schedule, keep on going, never stop

Master slain, his words in deafening rain
Only to fall where no one heard or abstained
Another down, generations round and back, again
Maybe this time pilots, blind, will lead the preying

Stranger Since Then

Where are you now
Last we met you were checking out
To other places than the ones my arms can fill

You had that look in your eyes, you were so lost
Just like the white swan took to the skies above, bearing its cross

Where have you been
You've been so vacant and distant
Out of my reach beyond the place I ever belonged

Wherever you are I wish you the best
Wherever you go I hope you live and love for the rest

When it all comes down kingdoms crumble to the ground
Keep standing for your pride and all that's left inside

Where have you come back from
It's been so long I almost didn't recognize you
I heard you like a bygone song

You have a different face for the very first time
A different look behind your eyes that speaks for days and goes on for miles

Dying For Fables And Myths

A fire to light the way, a poet with words to say
Everything that matters to us in the bitter end
A star that explodes on high, a reason to question why
Everything that shatters us has to ever end

This is it, the real thing in flesh and blood; it's not a dream
We are here for better, worse, or lost make it the best, for it came at a cost
This isn't exactly what we dreamed or what we saw in more ethereal scenes
This is what we've been given to live, stop dying for fables and worn out myths

A smile to lift your wings up off your back to fly
Spring up into the sky to live in the clouds and sing
A breath that will sweep you off the ground that used to be so soft
Losing it all is what we need to see who we are, who we were, and be free

When you're back on solid ground I'll be there and I'll come around
When your head is in the clouds you'll hear me speaking clear and loud
When you come back home you'll see everything wasn't what it seemed
When you open up your eyes the truth will light up all the lies

Ghost Towns Or Song

This useless ability to feel everything in the world
This broken machine limps on, tripping on all the cracks
These wandering masked facades stumble towards their destination

These noblemen tip their hats to invisible vagabonds

These makeshift halls stand alone, burying bones, gathering dust
Since good men stopped meeting here to stand and discuss
This old fox has lost its tale; it has no stories to tell
It's lived past its given life, unfortunately into mine, now up for sale

I've never seen so much activity in ghost towns or in song
I've never felt so alive in here, as when they've all finally gone

These winds blow all the words away by day through trees in the sound
Those lines in time's breeze are familiar; I've heard them spoken around
This old world gives way to us eternally
Whether or not we're ready to move along and shake off the rust and rot

Walking Ghost

Human tracks made in the snow
Where do they come from, where do they go
Two sets of tracks turn into one
They're on the shoulders of the favorite son

Taking life one day at a time
Life has its reasons even when it seems unkind
Living martyrs fighting off their wake
Theirs' is a strength that no one can take

What we call home is a palace to most
When you are living like a walking ghost
Still, with a smile they travel on more
To find their next stop and come to its door

Human tracks made in the snow
They're not alone – this is something they know
Outstretched hands and hearts come to their aid
When they need it most it won't be too late

Laying On The Grenade

I will lay on this grenade for you, I'll take the bullet if I must
I've done this for you so many times, in my disguises I do trust

I wear the mask so you don't see; you won't know I'm the one
Taking all the heat for you, I will not ruin your double-edged fun

When you see me passing by on some street recognize me when we meet
I'll be the one standing by, patiently, when you dodge the next one recognize it's me

I will take this punch for you so you can stay in the fight
I've seen you from a distance facing the long and lonely nights
I will take my place behind the shadows so I do not intrude
As you take the road you must to find the one awaiting you

Some day the time will come, sometime I will not be around
By then you'll be strong enough, the next shot won't take you down
Until then, you'll need me here in the corner of your eye
If you think see me, till the end, know that you are dear and mine

Pull Me From The Fire

When weakness gets the best of me I am my own worst enemy
I am the hand that pulls me down, following my own will to the ground
You've seen the heights I can climb when my heart and your words align
I've seen the past play in my head, movies of a man before he's learned to live again

And it's because of you

You pulled me from the fire; you picked me up off the ground
You lift me up and raise me high; when I least deserve it your love is mine

I've walked the path of least resistance, the long, hard road I have not won
In this endless cycle, circling around, another mile, another step, we'll move on
I know where I have been before, a life that stripped me to the core
I've been down on my knees more than once; I have a feeling I'll be there before I'm done

Angel Waiting In Wings

I've seen a glimpse of my future life and glimpses of my future wife
Though, I could not honestly tell you what either one looks like
I've seen previews of what comes next and almost know what to expect
Though, I could not honestly show you what's right in front of me

She's a child at heart, with a woman's touch; through her layers I see so much

With a spirit bouncing in and out, so alive she's burned into my mind
I'll have to wait for this to come to me, when it does, won't it be grand
I'll have to wait for this to come to pass, till then; we'll shift on like the sands

Fall Like A Car Crash

She lived her life on the stage
Everyday life was the name of this place
But I swore to her it didn't have to be a tragedy

Her fall from grace was more than documented over and again
But no one seemed to know the words that could have saved her life

They watched her fall like a car crash
They saw her live like a time bomb
They saw her grow up a child and become a sullen woman at odds

I saw her become an angel and watched the world pull her down
To its level out of spite and take its toll on her life

World In Motion

He put the world in motion and placed me here with you
He gave us hearts as deep as oceans
Why do we build walls to break through

He gave us days made for living and chose me for you
He gave us nights for forgiving
Have we forgotten what he lived through

The road wasn't easy
The victory wasn't cheap
The cost was a great life
We can only hope to redeem

He placed the world at our fingers and all the chances to be free
He put a name to all the faces
What are we so afraid to be

The road won't be easy
Victory won't come cheap

The life you leave is not forgotten
You simply have to believe

The story played out on the pages isn't always pretty and serene
But that's just to be expected
When it's all said and done we'll be freed

Earnestly Yours

In the end its winner take nothing
We're proud of everything we've got and everything we're not
The arrow wounds and shots

From the start it's a tragedy
We're thrown on stage
We're put on the spot to show what we're not and cast our hopes and lots

The bull in the ring is all around us, you see
Matadors only prance and swing capes
It's all a fine dance, motion of poetry with spear, sword, and lance

Then, back to familiar haunts and grounds
The same old taunts and crowns
All for nothing, more than thorns for soldiers weary, tired, and worn

Thoughts In The Small Hours Of The Morning

Rioters and writers; Christian lions brought to the fire
Broken lines and pulled up bootstraps spread all over territorial weather maps
Minds on fire a million miles away; bodies catching up to what mouths say
No time for reflection here, only checklists and quotas to clear

Come to see the show and pay the man at the door
It's only in the end we learn what it all was for

Words as weapons and threats as lessons
It's all done in a day's work and spent in one life's time
Not that we actually do anything worth watching
Seconds on clocks only tick by to words that rhyme

Leave out the way you came, but do leave it all behind

Don't try to take it with you; time is already out of sight and mind

Loose Connections

Poetry and lust are one in the same
They can't be tamed and when it pours it rains
Muses, they die, are reborn, and reprised
Into new roles they never thought they would find

Havoc and trust, purest when left alone to run a-bloody-mok
Leaving nothing, but everything, to chance
Rain and the flames douse and expire, run off, and rise up higher
Exploding into in the air; the land of no liars

Bones and old letters like days gone, but better, eternally tick and forever tock
Reminding us that the clock eventually stops spinning
Feathers and the night both take to flight, but not without leaving their mark
In the dark we see our true hearts

Judges and claws both have beady eyes and faces
Neither follow laws but the jungles', where no one ever leaves any traces

Words For Leather Bound Ears

I wrote a poem today
I'd like to read it you if you'd please not stone me
At least not alone

Thank you for your consideration

I read the first line
And you pulled a barb from a vine to bleed me
If only to slow me

Thank you for listening

I stopped reading and put them into a book, which nobody read
That's what they said
But they had enough material to trash me

Thank you for your time

I ran out of ideas when you wanted to see them
But it was already too late
I started another one

Thank you for patronizing me

And Then I'll Crawl

I've gone so far, but have not moved
Your vague perceptions are so misused
I've gained the world, but lost it all
It took all of a single moment
Your blind resentment is on the move

I am nowhere near where I was before then
Still, it seems that I'm stuck on it
I can't move, my feet won't budge
It took me out and left me for dead
The game has changed, am I what's left

Send me an angel with no anchors
No weight to bear, as mine is enough
Send me no angel with reasons, grudges, or cares
I'll carry on in stumbling steps until my fall
And then I'll crawl

I don't care for your looks or your eyes
Take them off me and find your own to ride
I don't find this place at home
In the clouds my thoughts still roam
With my feet still shackled in dirt

I don't expect you to understand
Only to give me space for my head
I don't expect any helping hand
To ever reach for me, again
You can't find what you don't know to look for

Send away all the angels from the choirs
There are no places for them here

Send me instead broken, brooding bearers
With chains just light enough to fly
And take me home

Mind Over Clatter

The lips didn't move, but I understood clearly
All that was meant behind the eyes
The movements were slow, focused, and apparent
Oceans of words are all too impairing

The form didn't change, but was dynamic just the same
The world, all around, wholly shuddered
Unsure how to fill all the space in
Between the form, so simply bold, and the chatter

Stolid in repose, unresponsive in its natural mode
Not deviating for any windfall or other
Brushing aside the mountains and tides
Since it all didn't even hardly matter

In time all the chimes will align with the signs
Spelling out the whispers among the clatter
The shaking of roots underneath all that broods
All the eyes, focused towards the clouds or ground, soothed

Pisces Heart

There's a child in this heart, a spirit that won't go away
There's a Pisces to this soul who's reeling, dreaming, escaping
Seeing things that no one else intuits, invisible and intangible, yet obstructing
All the lines I've drawn from here to there only to redraw the map and course

Life is easier this way and more true to form, beauty, and rhythm
The beat I hear is one you never will, not with that attitude, at least
Willfully I stumble on and gone, down my own path, on the run, again
Only, not from anyone or anything, just to make my destination in time

Channels For Ducks And Geese To Swim

They sold you broken bones again

The dice won't roll with skin worn thin
To watch you run the gauntlet for their many pretty friends

They taught their yes men to say no
To those of us who don't fit in
To suits with pieces so divided, always on the mend

We ride the fence, but we've made up our minds
To watch them live a lie on both sides, till they realize they're numbered
Drones, with clocks tick out their days

Parts fall off the great machine with no one looking back
Trails of obsolescence bleed to rivers where they wash away
All the while, we stand and wonder who's been keeping time

The few that made it off the line, the shipmates of despair
Cast into a sea of vultures screaming me, me, me

First to go were rational, spring-loaded heads
Then, went reasonable homegrown hearts
After that came loving revolt and rage, from well-meaning, tiny, damaged brains

Villagers with rocks threw first, then, ones with sticks hit next
After them, those who burned packed in heat, but lost it in the fire that put it out
What was left, but human pride or shambles of run-off shame in puddles

It was running down into drain pipes and pilling out into our free channels
For ducks and geese and fish swim on, to not worry about a thing

Call Me Judas

Quit striking me down with looks from across the room
I could have been over there by now
If you hadn't shot me down already
If you hadn't shot me down before

Don't make this harder than it is
I'm already losing my mind

Call me Judas, call me what you will
I don't always keep my word

Understand there are always a million thoughts
In my head at a single stance

Don't make me regret this again
I'm already losing my shine

I'm guilty of all this and so much more
But I'm making up for my sins
Don't write me off as an empty case
There's more to me beyond this skin

Quit breaking my stride before I get to walk
I could have been so far by now
Starting over is the hardest part
Harder than looking you in the eye

Calling Out To You

For all stars we've seen burn out there is another, waiting to take its place
For all the jesters in the court there is another, around the corner, with a joke on his lips
For every tear drop in the dirt there is an angel waiting in the wings
For every step we walk in stone there is an instigator around the bends we turn

We're running out of time and running out of space
We're losing precious moments and trying to save face

For all the grains of sand that blow away there is a hill to climb up now
For all the lives we save we lose our own, there is no reason to the rhythm we fall into
For every stand we take we block another path, there is no way to get around
For every map we have a match will burn, there's a reason why we're lost; never found

We've taken everything we can and only given what we choose
We've lost our souls for kitsch – we can only lose

I'm calling out to you
I'm calling out to you for help
I'm trying not to lose
I'm trying to lose everything I've ever had

As Far As I Can Tell

The clock hands turn violently from the ones to the twos
This comes more natural to the less and the few
Though nobody knows it now, most will come to find
Gravity is weaker than previously defined

Soldiers with hearts of gold are storming the fields
With life and love on hold they do as they wield
At home the spectators, with their glasses and wine
See what is happening, they sip and say that's fine

The telephone booths have ghosts with stories to tell
All it takes is one call and the toll of a single bell
Don't let them get too near or their words will become yours
Tours of duty here will be explained by the years

Boxes of memories, stored away tight
Collect memories of their own that stay out of sight
The last life I shared with you was enough for them all
But there is no end in sight as far as I can tell

Zeppelins Fall To Earth

When I don't love you anymore you will know if you don't know it by now
When your eyes don't hold your face at my attention your words give you away

This too shall pass – this too will fade away
It's never meant to last – it all fades away

When your zeppelins fall to earth your motives are no longer in the sky
When your wings, they shed their grace; at that moment you fell from the sun

So it's time to say so long to yesterday
What comes for us one and all, comes for us the same
So we're moving in our lines
Shuffle onward, till the wind blows nigh

When the time comes to travel on, to distant lands from where you've come
When my voice no longer sounds, like it used to, I will move on proud

Hat Box For A Pill Head

Their system fell apart today
The rich ones barked up a storm
This is the norm, they say

When the lights go out it's always the same thing here
No one around these parts knows what to do

They said it was something else political
Who can I trust today
That's all it ever seems to be

They're calling for a brand new hat
The one they've got just doesn't sit on top of the rack well anymore

Let them have their coup de tax, nothing changes anyway
Let their rivers fill with sand and lead, a rain will come along to wash it all away

All the boxes hold the same old hats
They just sit on different heads
Or so it seems to me

All the matches flicked at once
Sparked a smoke screen, just enough for the senators to escape

Ideal Boy

There he goes over the edge again
Full of bright ideas that will change the world
If they do not kill him first

On the move in circles, once again
Spinning out of control
Tying knots into the rope didn't help him hold on

Taking on the greatest villains, standing up to modern giants
Wasn't in the plans for this one
Not this timed soul

Sailing into waters over his head
For a great ideal that gets drowned amidst the waves
Of negative creeps come out to play

Taking hits at walls that surely will not fall for ages
Knowing what he's done was pure
Even if no one else knows

With a stone to fight Goliath
Knowing he's the underdog, still, he holds his battle lines
Till he's overrun or the day was won

This Scene Is Over

Sweet lyric, my dear cynic, your letters open up my eyes
No distance can diminish your words or how I see you smile

The world is changing and so must we
You're always so sarcastic, the way we've got to be

Magnificent Delilah, you're right out of an old book, true
Right down to the happy plaything you take with you to kill your blues

This scene is over; let's make one of our own
For those that follow, let the others leave us alone

I'm throwing in the towel; I've already lost, today
The moon hasn't even risen, it's still bright and sunny, oh hell

Fragments And Lapses

Bible belt dealers in heresy shake in their skins
Monocled hunchbacks with canes as legs know when they're pinned
As scoundrels and crooks and freemasons all wear the same looks
Knowing what drives them on, mocking everyone below

Grasping for straws, all the drowning men see where they've been
Momentary lapses in blindness on occasion creep in
Fragments of blue-green sky, a flash in the pan, this is it
The moment of epiphany we are all stuck in

What comes next is for all philosophers to argue
Meanwhile, on the home front everyone else lives their lives
Yells of the drunken ones piercing my windows at night

Good for them, they have found God and he's way out of sight

Pictures of me and my previous wonderful deeds
Eclipse anything that I've done ever since these shirtsleeves
Who knows the words that we mean to say in our hour of need
Blinders for you and me make this much easier to see

Maskils And Psalms

In maskils and psalms I've learned all I need to know
The right and the wrong, how to burn bridges all day long
Back in the day foxes in henhouses ran the show
All the old machinery brought down from the mountains ran so slow

Parables history has told, lost forever as time moves on
Even though characters come and go the bonds between magnificent creatures grow

All the paper leaves trails across the great, wide desert sands
Where the journey took place, chugging on like ships unmanned

When the radar has failed your crew is off the map
Wandering, wondering happily, following lines made by sticks and staffs

Emissaries Of Perdition

All of the emissaries from their distant lands
By their nature, needy, letting go of delegated demands
Sheep in wolves' clothing, not so awe inspiring
When you get down to it all, simple players in the cloth

As for all the parading floats for miles, money down the sink
Breaking all the precepts we thought they should be
Pearls for the swine, imagined so to bring out their eyes
In the end tend to only bring out their false smiles

For all of their career pining, whittling matches out of fog
In delirious visions they think they'll save the world
Such a vulgar notion to take on the world
Still, someone must do it, why not them, after all

Set up tables for the masses to lean on while they wait

For the spectacle of villains, a grand human showcase
One will stand out different than the masses' formula
Bringing change, maybe perdition, let's hear the verbal podium brawl

Fashionably In

With the wolves out open up the stalls
All the pens and cages; let all the feelings out
Verbal spillage, cathartic at best
Heals all the wounds, cleans up all the mess

Confessing for ages of human err and sin
Giving up the ghosts, now, is fashionably in
Winding up the jack boxes, twisted thoughts and gears
Apply the brakes and slow down to mend up all the tears

Blowing out the candles too quickly is a shame
We've missed out on games children taught us to save
Tending to ourselves; sitting down to the meal
Breathe in, once again; there is no need of swords and shields

Waltz

We're alone, now; at least that's how it feels
All the miners are done digging for the day
Sleeping babies show us how to be
When ideas and vision escape us momentarily

The tender evening comes on
Like a rite of passage for all ages alight
We've been locked out of the bars, but the stars are bright
There are no windows here, only endless, cloudless eyes

Blinking skyways making us feel small
Next to giants and everything else in flight
Here, the final waltz is only the beginning
There is no last dance, only interrupted dreaming

The Grey Matter Jones

She was jonesing for more than the dim lights could offer

More than overhead fans banded together
When the microphone was still open the room was full
There was music in the air and poetry spoken

She gave up the ghost at the corner of the bar
To study grey matter and other things from afar

There was an ounce of sadness, but a gallon of relief
When the lady resurfaced, still cool and serene
Nothing has changed since, though the plot of land is empty
Missing the spark that came so plenty

When you move on you've left all but what you can't take with you
Memories and microphone stands, voices still heard clear and true

The story is over, the taste out of your mouth
The jonesing will be no more, that's the newest fair

The Ghost In The Details

Grey water is surrounding all that remains unsaid
The digital age has territorialized the sand
The shifty-eyed gazes from across the room
Tell me what's happened to everyone way too soon

The roots don't run so deep; the tracks aren't laid so far
To pierce into the ages beyond our reaching arms
The wounds cut much closer, too close to the heart
What matters and doesn't gets confused right from the start

The ghost in the details has given up on itself
No longer even trying to defend what it sells

I'll Come Back

This is the regular fare; this is how it goes down
When you're running on air that eventually runs out
We're the average of the odds, the best chances to take
Way up in the sky for no one else's sake

This is the standard operating procedure to follow

To go down the rabbit hole, maybe this time for good
This is a fine collection of atrocities you have
When you think of something better to show me, then I'll come back

Tired Lays Of Track

I've seen your writing on the wall
I've heard your words spoken in the halls
Thrown about the crowd before, to land on deaf ears

I've dug your image from the books
I've dug your vibe and your hooks
In the company of fools and vagabonds who will never understand in time

Still, we keep etching new words in the ledgers and notebooks
Still, we batter down doors with guitars in their cases
And stigmas on our back

We've been in this together
For so long it seems too hard
To believe it's been that long, but it has anyhow

We've faced the leather-eared masses
The tin-minded souls with nothing behind their eyes
Blissful fools all in rows

We'll keep on chugging down this tired lay of track
Until something sticks to the wall and sends us letters back

Allegory Of Unrest For The Empty Spaces

We are the standouts in a crowd that is thinning
The lines are blurring – the herds are thinning
You were the bright spot in the room full of shadows
The only things that mattered were the mystical hollows

What could you see there
What could we be there
Who cold think clearly
With such a lack of noise

I was the loner in a breadline of followers
The talking in circles and lines ceased to be with me
We haven't changed much, the roads with shiny pavement
Seem, still, just as bumpy as they were before

We were the stars, then
We were the show's end
They never got us
We knew they'd never understand

Creditors And Horsemen

They're sitting on their high horse thinking themselves to death
Giving away their fortunes that are already spent
We're here, a good distance far away from where the action is going down
No matter to us, anyway, it doesn't affect us, anyhow

They're envisioning their master plan, the one that trumps them all
That gives way to some other monsters they won't be able to tame

Their glasses tinkle silently; their slaves are in the fields
It's all in their heads, anyway; it's not real, anyhow

They're planning the contingency, getting ready to lock down
Nailing down all the furniture they don't want swept away

Our Small Pond

I'm happy to report all is well and all is good
The vultures are no closer than the grounds where we once stood
Statuaries of the greatest day tell the stories we don't lament
It's brighter seeing it this way, than to idle on memories spent

The court clerks and statisticians with their pencils and pads in hand
Will soon be out of work, now, when grim-faced reports aren't in demand

I'm satisfied with our place in the big picture where we stand
Small fish in a small pond, barely visible on the map

History may forget us, though we will always matter most
With a ghost of a chance, now, of raising up a toast

Riot squads and special policemen can all put down their shields
The chatter won't be bullets, but rather, words we won't conceal

Speaking big words won't be needed, flashing bulbs, nor neon signs
Pomp and circumstance is overrated when there's no need for them, or time

Scrabbling

Some waste away to skin and bones, some wear smiling masks when all alone
In the corner of the bedroom the chair keeps rocking long past the stories final word
Some clocks keep ticking in fallen towers; some thoughts don't slow down after hours
In the perfect moments we don't think; all on their own time and place just meet

I'm trying to find the words to say what can't be said
I'm trying to write a melody to make the quiet moments sing

Filling in blanks is not that easy when the choices are too many
So I put one foot in front of the other and make my way to where I know

Some know the things that keep us busy; some move and shake the world spinning
In my head poets write till they're wearied by all the weight of what they've found
Some drift along like ships at sea, some fly so high their wings move free
In dreams the visions come, not blurry, instead, they're clear as bells and mirrors

You may see things a little different, what's held between four walls always is
Either way, we always make it back to the place where we were found

Preachers, Boots, and Brothers

Preacher man from across the table
Knows how to be and what to do
Saves my soul over dinner
And sometimes over coffee, too

He stays sharp and keeps me in his prayers
God knows I need it, too
He's off to speak to the people
The good words he knows are true

Boot country family tries to fatten me up
Like a turkey before Thanksgiving, to be trumped

I know a skinny man is a frightening thing
But don't you worry a moment about me

Always invited, never able to be the host
One day it will be the other way around
For now I do this thing called music and poems
Real life is lost on me; I'm out of the loop for miles

Brothers and sisters, mothers and fathers gather round
I've got a word to say about what's going down
I don't have faith in much beyond what I can believe
Lucky for everyone I see the glass is very deep

One going against the grain is bound to make a scene
That's all right with me; I know this world is mean
I'll make my rounds until the great eyes finally blink
I could wish for more than this life, so I think

Treads In Rounds

Open up the window, pull the shade and get real quiet
Can you hear the murmur trying to play it real sly
Throw open the door – turn the lamp down low
You can see the flicker, the electric air current it rides

Leave me tomorrow or leave a note today
Telling me where you went, either way, it's all the same
Swing high dull chariot, move to the side
Can you see it coming straight for you, banging on division bells in time

No more regressing since this came around
Sound off the war drums, it feels too right
The church is now people, with buildings burned to the ground
No sight is unholy; they leave no treads, but make their rounds

Bow String

Starry-eyed little wonder, stealing the thunder from the clouds
Innocence so captivating I could pick you out of a crowd
Playing on blue moons and phosphorescence, falling everywhere around her head
Incredible is the sound she makes when the bowstring moves and sways

Fill the room with music, haunting melodies in rounds
Circling back for another time, again, to make their sound
The guitar plays off in the distance, not to be outdone all at once
Still, it only takes one moment, another melody, stealing its way in, comes

Stand up with me, take your bow
Stand up alone, now, this one's for the crowd, they are yours
It's getting hard to focus, losing oneself inside the drone
Melancholy to the bones of it bringing one final note home

I play my part like a shadow; I'll take the backseat for now
While I'm just one of a million, look around, she can't be found
Render me voiceless, not so much as a sound
Keep me suspended, still animated, but not bound to this earth

Story Of An Expatriate Of Something

Making my rounds in the rye, catching what I can, here and there
Never quite able to follow just one trail, committed to noncommittal
An expatriate of something, but what

Leaving no trail of breadcrumbs, Hansel, not so much, neither Gretel
I seek no house of candy or witches, only something to fall back on
I'll know it when I see, but where to look

I'm far from captain of this ship; no white whale defines my direction
There's no Ishmael to call me otherwise, only a kid with dreams in his hands
And somehow, trails of past ice cream cones on his face

There's no Odysseus with battle plans drawn, no Trojan horses or trap doors set
Great paved seas, however, do lie before me, no vast army of friends have I enlisted, however
After all, who can keep track of so many

I've never brought fire from the Heavens, Prometheus-sized feats won't be seen
Still, I look to the clouds for something, bound or unbound, thy will be done
While my own becomes unraveled

Fables, I have spun, in the many, true to Aesop and his forest, it's all fair
Much more than simply fun and games, still, it's all only up in the air

Till it comes down all over the floor

Sticks will be picked up, stones never bothered to be thrown
I have gone by many names before, I still have much more left and there's more to come
Until then, they haven't quite won

All I Need

The way you regarded me, so unceremoniously
Almost drove me to never come back and just leave
If not for the good ones, the ones that I do all this for
There would be no more, I wouldn't find my way to your door

All I want is a little appreciation, just to know I'm not doing this in vain
All I want is a little understanding so I know that you just may feel the same

I can overlook them, the ones that never understood
What it takes to stand out and put yourself on the limb
As long I can be pretty sure that you will still come back around
At least to pop your head in and make your presence known

When I see your face, again, know that it makes me feel all right
Hearing your voice through the crowd gives this all meaning, makes the mood light

If You Pass By, Wave

Up late, again, trying to find my motivation, be it good, be it bad, or in between
Lost hours, no matter, what's the big deal if I find it in the end
Train whistle blows off in the distance; they're going somewhere, ahead full speed
Leaving tracks they can't deny behind, no matter here, secrets blow in the breeze

I'll make my way to where I'm going, come hell, high water, all the same
You'll see me at the end of the line, if you pass by, at least wave

I found myself, again, in a spot like this, sometimes it feels tighter than before
I always make it out, some way or another, who knows why or what for
They're charging forward, never stopping, eyes on the target, all along
Fearless for want of something glorious to be remembered in poem or song

Something Real, Not A Ghost

These desperate haunts I will no longer attend
Empty shells of broken men, women just as empty float around, too
Those dim lights aren't for mood; they cover up what everybody is hiding
As if it won't find its way as far into the light as it can go

People robed in depression, faces trying to hide what's underneath
Washing down bittersweet sustenance – bottles, emptied, still don't bring relief
I've never been their captain and I won't go down with that ship
My hands were made for holding, not for strangling out nervous sweat or bottled thieves

Who will take their leave with me and would rather take the chance
Facing down tracks going somewhere, instead of the same old, tired dance
I am not without pity; just don't expect me to carry them all
I'd much sooner be dragged down with them and lose my ability to walk, let alone crawl

Show me more behind your eyes; you will beckon my attention most
And keep my gaze locked onto you, something real, in the flesh, not a ghost

Portents And Stories Retold

Ghost ships on dry land, like what we had in small portions, spent
Rumrunners from days past, still, in the game for what it's worth, I guess
Zephyrs and hurricanes both come in and leave with mythical speed
Statues and dolls all look back with eyes that know what they've seen

It was red, it was white, and it's always different as night and day
Storm damage and rain both wash a slate clean through a path of pain
First mates and seconds hands play second fiddle yet demand the same
Lines in the horizon and stars in the sky have written the stories we retell in our minds

Time To Run

You call this your setting sun; mine hasn't even begun to rise
We both see things differently, this, to me, is no surprise
You see castles to the sky; I see a place to lay my head

That's all right with me; just keep my head above water
As long as I can see what's coming and still have time to run
Sweep aside the weights and chains; so much dust is on the shelf
Leave the past like picture frames hanging where it stands

Drown the voices in your head and little figurines with creepy faces

What can I say to that, your words were so well spoken
You closed up the book you were feverishly writing

The final statement set in stone, nothing bears repeating

Soapbox Witticisms

The air up there, it is no fancier
Prison walls all the same, still tall
Cobble roads are just as bumpy uptown
As the misty marshes' water falls

The pavement is always gray as slate
Fenced in yards, still just as easy to climb
Criminal minds were always masters of destiny
Reason's always reasonable; some words always rhyme

You may have ribbons and bows
Streamers may line your streets in rows
Parade your words, your phrases, and soapbox witticisms
Vanity and its bounds are still unknown

Thin Air And Lost Time

Guitar case in hand he made his next move
He's on his own, he decided, not needing these fools
They like the dim lights and same old songs
They could go on for hours saying nothing new

Give them their dark rooms and times gone past
Let them fall into the same scene, once again
Their play has the same cast and only one act
It all comes around, no question of where and when

The man in the parking lot says, "Don't go away,
We're only getting started"
I know you mean well, but you don't understand
Just where my heart is

Getting home, across the street, he opened up his book
About expectations larger than his own
By a writer from ages past and distant
Still, they shared the same dream for a moment

"I'm going to find my time to shine,
But you're wasting mine, for now" he said
"Good riddance, either way,
 It was never personal in the end"

Like a prisoner in the night he made his plans
While he was still free, one day to be in demand
"I'm only biding my time here or till this works out"
He said, knowing if it didn't at least he tried

"I'll try again some other time, but not right now"
He said to himself knowing what was on his mind
Reaching for the stars is worth it in the end
Even if all you pull back is thin air and lost time

Debtors And Artistic Criminals

The pressman was a vampire by virtue and by trade
The working, waking hours broken up by tentative dreaming, just the same
Downtime was an illusion when the lines keep running, from you, away
Almost like it was wartime carrying on for our souls to be saved

The writers and the poets all have enough words with which to say
Everything that could be said for years, months, weeks, and days
Working at their writing tables, trying to stay just below broke
Here's the joke, it's all futile, to be visionary above the grave or fires stoked

Debtors and artistic criminals like us would have been imprisoned long ago
But for the sake of someone or something we're made to perish in our heads, all alone
I don't know what's worse, shackles on our ankles or bills stacked high
Pretty soon they'll block out our only view, through the window to the outside

The Outliers

When the stage collapses and souvenir stands get torn down
When it happens on perfect axis in synchronized time

All hands on deck shuffle, scattering like burnt ants
Pawns, jokers, queens, and kings are equals; muffled screams turn into chants

It's time to tell stories, now, the fair and the bold
They've all earned their name in print, a strong, solid voice once crowed

When the coaches fall silent and the field-play all stops
Follow divots in the cold dirt; take time to see how we've been robbed
All the drivers with hand whips have no horses left to tame
They've gone their own direction, isn't it always just the same

When the circus tent shakes wildly from all the action inside
Fortune telling stands dwindle, along with indecisive outliers

Static On The Radio

The static on the radio plays the sweetest lullabies
Let's put to rest all the myths that white noise is dead
The wind on the carried breeze whispers secrets we know
All to remind us in the end where to go from here
The past days cling to my back, though they don't see the light
Looking forward into the sun the magnificent night comes on

Arrested Development And Donated Time

Turn the music up and the voices down
I want to hear what you're all about
Set the radio free from the fake formulaic dreams
With no sight, no vision to be found

We're all stars when we're broke
When we're children at heart
With everything to give
All we ask for is a start

We've set our goals high and set some low
When we fall in the middle we've found ourselves
Though nobody knows what's on our minds
No matter how many times they ask us, oh well

We'd rather have living recognition than yours

A room full of ragdolls is empty as hell
More lonely than a canvas with no room for any more
Where nobody knows what's beneath the shell

Arrested development within donated time
Walking on broken glass on nobody's time
I never want to leave the real world behind
But sometimes I still want to step away

My Secret Sharer

My secret sharer, I never knew I had a twin
I'd never wish to put this on anyone
We lived separate lives before, only as an affront
Now, we see the truth of it laid bare

My darkest ally resembles me down to the last
For better or worse who can suppose to know
Nothing is known of you apart from what's known of me
Who's to even begin to suppose

My ghost in plain sight, driving me insane
You can only hide so long before you've got to go
When my soul is pulling other directions from within
I know something is wrong, I believe

This Seems About Right

I didn't know what to say to you so I didn't write
I didn't know how to stand up so I didn't fight
You don't know how to respond to me so you didn't speak
You never knew how to take me so you didn't even leave

The safety of our little worlds is contagious
Opening our doors is way too hard
We just might let too much of the outside world in
And wouldn't that just be the end

They never knew how to handle us so they packed up and moved on
They always thought we were strangers so they left their lights on
The others saw us from a distance so they never came closer

The others were always skeptical so they wrote us

The sweetness of our own confines is illusory
It isn't always quite what we see
The freedom of a life without chains in scarier
Then being raised upon hands and knees

If you don't want my heart on my sleeve just throw this all away
Others will find me lying there and take me for a ride
Where this goes I've never known and don't care to
As long as I'm on the move I'm far from dead

You can't kill me
You can't even try
You never thrilled me
This seems all too right

<u>Rats In A Scrum</u>

The successful psychopath became a millionaire
With shifty gazes from eyes he smiled
Looking out onto the masses through his grin
Dressed, superficially speaking, in designer lies
The well-meaning poet got shot down, again
He's currently freezing, left out in the cold
Maybe if he were more ruthless he'd be acceptable
If only he had it in him to lie

No one wants a feeling man around
Just stuff it in the closet to fester and drown
Carry on with empty eyes in your head
To please the one's who'll never understand

The dictator dictated letters to his secretary
Telling the people how they should feel
With a strong-armed bodyguard on his hip
Standing much taller than he seems
The charitable blackmailer smiles sweetly
When his face isn't wrinkled up into a snarl
His hand on the button to start the panic mode
For when he's feeling insecure

No one wants the honest man with mild delusion
Stemming from hope to give this meaning
Meanwhile, they stomp their feet retreating
From anything that requires feeling

Run, everybody run, here comes the flood
Cornering us trapped rats in the scrum
Hide, everybody hide, somewhere deep inside
They can't get you there, at least not yet

Squares And Logarithms

I don't fit into your squares and logarithms
I can see behind your eyes you've lost faith in me
So put it into words and just say it
Let's not play this old game and charade

I've cut many a tie from the old lives
What's one more if it means nothing at all
I've walked on and never turned to look back
At the wake of devastation and tragedy

You can keep your eyes narrow and the words within your lips
I bet you never knew I didn't need those signs to see the truth that exists

What's new with the old ways and habits
Is nothing worth repeating, it's all the same
What's left is a shell, an empty compliment
You could have kept those words to yourself

I see with mine eyes and hear with mine ears
What's beyond and between the lines
I see with my heart and feel with my soul
Reading past the pages into the spine

They can fill me up with phrases and the words can stack up high
I bet they never knew I saw through it, to the meaning inside

Here's One

Here's one for the record books, the hero that went into battle with creeds
No sword, horse or shield in hand, defending himself with spoken words on his knees
Here's one for the obvious, the reasons for everything has been leaked
No secrets remain about anything, it's all whispered in breezes through trees

The sound from the factory, the explosion of machines
Couldn't unrest the weakest of these, it didn't awaken the breeze

Here's one for the thinker, Rodin's head, what's on your mind is nothing new
It's all been said before so many times, what's original is so far and few
Here's one for the broken down roadside, all the traffic passing by is just like you
All going somewhere way to fast, just to find another moment was breezed through

The clank of the engine parts rusted from years of exposition
Eventually the bolts all fall off, part of their club with small inclusion

Jumping Ship

With their cursory glances and thoughts left to spare
Put tires to the ground, now to get away from their fare
For all the half-loaded compliments do you mean what you say
For the next line that's uttered kicks against what you brayed

With your one-sided commentary and your shortsighted vows
Close your ears to their madness and empty wolf howls
For all the charm and charisma you have faked all the way
Do you not see through the veneer for all your moral decay

I'm jumping this ship, we're already flooded, mates
Their humanity is weighing us down and holding us back for days
I'm leaving this town, for the ones riding the horse
No longer see straight, now, but only follow their blind course

The Straightjackets Collapse

It's all starting to sound the same in my head
All the faces and sidewalks roll into one
The borders between go on for miles
The gatecrasher's party has just begun

Still, I don't quite find myself minding the distance

There's comfort in the gaps and spaces in between
I almost enjoy knowing you can't just waltz in
And up-end everything I just set in place

The shelled in and hell bound make their way
Hemmed in on all sides, but beneath
Still, their ground seems to tremor and quake
Ceaselessly jarring their compasses around

Others scream vacancy at the top of their lungs
They've proven, again, to be no fun in different tongues
We're taking it all as if it couldn't be wrong
Some bought into the stock and sold the whole farm

It's happening too fast
The buckles and snaps
This used to feel so familiar
Till the straightjackets collapsed

A Sagittarius On Tuesday

You're not from this town, that's what I dig about you the most
You're not from around the way far or near
You're drawn by the sound of works spoken poetically
Never broken or found to be in a condition haphazardly

The lost and the drowned are both more than we'll ever be
The roads and crowds are driven on forward forever
The fossils and crowns both age with a grace most astounding
The dukes and the counts both off by a little, keep watch

We're drawn to this place with pencils held by dignitaries
We're freelance and starved with a glut of compassion carrying
We're both moving on – the boundaries are nonexistent
We're souls full of clowns, the show for the world to see

Graffiti and Aviary Giants

Graffiti walled castles, coffee stained wooden tables
Stand against the storm leaning on a sketchy resume
Aviary giants hover, disjointed words and phrases

Muttering airborne optimism, pessimists all over cringe

Broken down wrecks, necks craning stand one-legged
Baggage carried on carousels sees more miles than we ever will

Make sense of this stream, nonsense swims carelessly
Raging tides swell and crash, getting nowhere with big noise
Worse for the cause are the rushed words and antimatter
The best in show classifying ventriloquists true to themselves

The Middle And Sometimes The End

It began at the middle and sometimes the end
The first words are always the forgettable kind
The starting gun was shot off out of time, so it was done
In a kingdom of false starts the emperor was on the run

It began with a whisper, though we only registered the bang
The early were forgotten, minus the reenactments that always came
It was all for the actors and actresses to get their feet in the door
The one who caused it to be open was forgotten once more

The middle times aged and evil time self-medicated
In deep meditation it all ran afoul, but still worked, instead
The steeped mysticism gathered up in the clouds raining down
When it rained it poured till the people were all washed out

The middle of the story was told with twisted plots all intertwined
When they're fresh in your mind briars always seem to grown on vines
In his epiphany's moment the crowd was on break, they missed it all
There went the only proof that had any stock or hold, all to fall

The end of the track is always coming on down the line
In the flourish of carousel distractions, disjointed, no one seems to mind
It wasn't till the game was halfway over when they saw the light
When persuasiveness dims and indecision runs thin who is in the right

The end always is, but the book says it never will be or was
When the trips around the track drag out we say differently and increasingly pause
It's always the same; they'll give interviews till they're blue, how they knew this one
When they didn't see a thing all along, but their own biased could-be, it was already done

Harvesting Identical Ones

They hid in plain sight; they did it on the back page
Between the unwritten lines and unchecked spaces
The secret of life, evaluation, and blankness
Hiding loose-ended grins in open, tangled up sentences no one blessed

All the daughters in the sun had male children's fun, all the while hoping
Out where the boys fear to tread around the women, stories, lore, and folk
It was fun when it all was a game, but seriousness came, blowing it wide open
The lids on the cans, unruly demands, we're on a roll over uneven sides

The changes in plans no one saw coming with their eyes all closed
In the pews and rows the vows went untold, though we all knew
Where thin air stands solid and walls crumble down it was obvious
No one would see or even be around for it all, one last attendance

Holing away for tomorrow all of today seemed to be a great ideal
When the dirt got turned up so did all of their stuff and blew away
The faintest clear notion seemed hollow enough to float on water
Still, it doesn't have legs on which to stand above drowning sea level

To put it all into focus I see with eyes that stare at the sun
And speak with a tripping rhythm stumbling over itself
Down time, broken parts put together all make up the sum
Collecting till we're full, ready to burst, and be done

A Door With A View

If you stare at the walls hard enough you will find me
Right next to the dispensers of salt for the earth
Winding and snaking my way to finding an exit
Though only my eyes are moving for the door

If you look hard enough at the grandeur of the long view
You might understand what will be said next
Read between all the lines and the blank spaces
Then get out of my head before it gets too strange

If the glare from the sun is too much then stop getting distracted

By the spots in its skin that come with its age
We all burn out sooner or later, eventually speaking
And go out the only way that's acceptable, the way we came

If another ride down this road seems too heavy for the soul
Feel free to ride on the back of the pack beast in the stall
They're perfectly built for this place; they'll surpass us all
Unfeeling enough to stay sane, staying blind strictly by choice

If terms of the speaking kind are too much to bear turn the handle
Let the blood that runs through your veins be mine no more
It seems that my type may be too heavy to carry, even on the move
The next order of business is finding a door with a view or a window

The Nature Of Collisions

While trying to recover the previously lost ships I have found
I've succeeded only in smothering all the sands that shifted around

While flying kites in remembrance of the souls that are still bound
I've only caused the past to be dug up and the memories to be drowned

While burning all the manuscripts by dead writers in the ground
I've freed the spirits on the pages, releasing all the caged up hounds
While burying the evidence, stuffing treasures deeper down
I've broken things wide open, making all the more of sound

Plot twists in all directions; one trick ponies lead the way
Avalanches down the mountainsides, ripping and tearing the tops astray
Fearing everything we don't know throws wide the door to even more
Ravens flap in ever cawing, like we just gave away the store

Landslides in the compress run over the edges we're trying to hold
Proving nothing to the watchers in the night, hiding because they're sold
As days turn into nights, now, locks spin in their chairs
Though nailed down in one position, while the daylight climbs the stairs

As the wheels rotate, miles pass under the carriage riding by
Hovering over the lines they're following, two by two and side by side
As lodgings turn into mausoleums we're more consistent everyday
Getting a little more predictable, once moving traffic tends to stay

As chrome no longer carries the baggage it used to sell
Out of the back of salesmen's wagons traveller's souls were likely felled
Riding high on superstitions the cloaked men held long vigil
In the presence of the cowering masses, who stare on standing still

All the while the homes are empty, but for the scavengers in the walls
Coming out to count the seconds and feed on what's left in trough
Finally, leaves turn over madly, changing hands, one to the next
As the grass starts brand new cycles nature is taking back over, what did we expect

A Cross Between Two Men

Look at how you've evolved, now, not a day late or short
Over the limit isn't in your blood, right on the money, fortunate son
You've never much cared for fairy tales or hard luck stories they've told
Making heads or tales of two-sided parable tends to go quick and get old

It never gets any easier for those like us it's on par
For the course we're trudging down seems to always move uphill
Never satisfied is your calling card, one thing you'll take to the grave
Still, smiling, seeing through it all, while you're on your way

You're not a sucker for a bleeding heart that mends a little too quick
Especially when it's got you in its claw range or grip
It's always on the move, for us the game is hard to catch
Like catching light in a bottle it's trying to get it to stick

Volume One Of Many

The great divide widens
The will we must follow, it waits
In hiding, for the right amount of time
Before coming out to play

The masses flow like water
The oil never mixed in well
In cases like this that's for the better
Sometimes you can't quite close the sale

I'll never write another love song

As long as I have breath
Or a steady hand of purpose
Over the pencil's craning neck

The breathless wait for something
The wailing voices go up to the sky
In other circumstances, more frightening
Seem light through my mind's eye

The gaps and spaces in between tell the stories
The lines between, they've never read
In so called empty places we hide
What only few are let to see

I'll never let my guard down, anytime soon
He'll stay on duty, no change of shift
Only gleams of light can pass through
Glimmers of light, allowed, get in

The writing goes on till it seems wrong
The run-on words and people get stopped
In here it all makes so much sense
To cut the rattling on right off

The understanding souls are left to be
The misunderstood ones may roam
In clear confusion, as long as need be
Till they leave and go back home

I'll never defend a king in battle
But my principles stand strong
You'll never get the whole of my attention
Unless it was meant to be all along

Fall Out, Stage Hand

Slack jawed aristocrats on hand
Delivering speeches off the cuff
Like sand to the desert, words are spread
Making their way in every crack and seam

They won't be able to get it all out later on
No amount of cleaning the skeletons out
Can clear the tracks and impressions made
It was more photogenic at the time of conception and shame

Now, where do we stand on the stage
To the left or right, the crowd harangued
Ears only bend so far till they break
Words hang in the air longer than we care

Stuttering criminals make their statements
Even smooth tongues come undone
Go along for the ride to see what happens
If you're so bored, just don't get taken

Jumbled assemblies of atrocities pile up
They're harder to carry stacked so high
The weight is more crushing to the feeling
Than to the dead, creepily smiling, inside

Now, where do we land after the fallout
The soft and the hard both can break
Points of attachment seem more a target
Out in the open anything seems fair

The Character Of Brother Henry, Mr. James

Though the man, the corporeal body, is gone
I will give you perfect immortality
I will remember your life, read your words
Complete your thoughts, study your form

It matters not where these words were epiphanied
And less where they were written
And even less, the time and date the deed was done
Only that they were regarded to live on

Though time marches on to ticks of clocks
Though dates are marked off on calendars
Though words spill forth from mouths everyday, in a flood
All that matters is that you are remembered

It's not measured in multitudes and throngs
Or numbers of words in books and critiques about you
It's not recorded in hash marks, scratches, in stone or sand
Only in the indelible minds that never cease to delve deeper

Phantoms of days gone past may rest here
Wearing all the amulets we bestow upon them
It's only that, and how, we receive them
That's all that matters, brother Henry, Mr. James

Till then we'll keep on turning screws
Till then we'll keep on turning up daisies
Till then we'll keep writing portraits
Portraits of doves' wings, ambassadors, and on

Ballad Of The Working Class Factory Gentlemen

The dancing mechanic does his routine on the factory shop floor
For the judges and beholders to watch and hold up their scores
Yay, from all, is what he usually hears without any to-do
It's all part of the regular shift, the working hours wearing away soon

The Irish Ivy League-schooled gentleman pacing round and round
Taking a piece of the action from here and there without a sound
Driver's cap on his head, wiry mop shooting out
He's the picture a mad scientist, Einstein, in his silence he shouts

The methodical Everyman, planning his steps throughout the day
Moving no faster than one's notice, still going a long, long way
A little banter with the passer-byes is always in store
Till he fires up the scene and sparks proceed the show

The rough edged sympathetic who pass off as more
Wearing the clothes of a Hell's Angel, but a gentlemen, nothing short
Never says an unkind word, does his day's dues, and gets paid
Never seeking applause or recognition, simply keeping his chi safe

The lead man with the agenda and priorities in hand
Always on the move somewhere, sure to be off as soon as land
Calling out for back-up, reporting in with the stats

Keeping cogs, paper, and people all in order, while wearing many fine hats

They young Herculean spinster, throwing words around like Ali
With a peace never shaken, like Mohamed or the Buddha, you see
Quick wits, no non sequitors, fly off the shelf of his tongue
He's the man of the people, on the move up, never to be outdone

What Do 5 Bars Of 12 Blues Make

Pass me hammer; pass me a nail
Don't ask me how, but I've got to bust a man from jail
Pass me those nuts; pass me those bolts
Other than you everyone I know is a criminal or a dolt

Pass on me now or pass on me later
Just don't get too involved if you can't stand my company for a while

Give me some change; give me some tips
On how to live a clean life free from sneaks and drips
Give me some oil; give me that can
I've got a creaky joint, but I need to escape from that man

Give me what you can, I won't ask for more
I'll get it back to you someday when I get paid

Change places with me; change your mind, too
Then, we can be the same person as me and you
Change what you think; change what you know
Just as long as you don't go too far from home or crawl too low

Change in a jar; change in bucket loads
Nothing ever changes anyways; it just turns from new to old

Break that old habit; break out of that mold
The one that you've been cast, rehashed, used, and sold
Break in a new soul; break a leg for me, too
Just don't do it on stage, I'm trying to get ahead of you

Break a promise if you have to; break your back for your pay
Just don't bend for anything that blows in the wind

Pick up sticks; pick up a brand new habit
Give it back in the end, then claim that another nabbed it
Pick out a new wardrobe; pick your friends while you still can
In the end pretend to be a loner and start a solo band

Pick a horse in the race; picket signs all point the way
We're all going south, anyways, at least some day

Public Surface Judgment

The shrine has been built, but it wasn't given a face
It's out of place here in this time, but no one knows why
It could be because of karma or the moment was wrong
Could be it just wasn't meant to happen this time around

The statue holds a firebrand and a winning smile
All the while people stand around to slowly admire
Some say it's so bold - others say it's cold and heartless
Either way, it will stand for a long time to come

The gravestone was dubbed an American name, quite graciously
There was no inscription to read, but a date stamped clear
For ten years in the future - now why would anybody do that
It was part of some master plan whose planner no could find to ask

The door hanger says everyone is out, but the lights are still on
There's a man inside, though - I can hear its shadow hum
The tune it sings is quite sad, so I guess the sign is true
No one knows what you've been through till they've been there, too

The letter's address says 'Go To Anywhere Else But Here'
It's clear to me someone's on the move very soon
I wonder if it was a bad debt or drastic change of heart
We'll all know in a few weeks when the airmailed postcard gets lost

The book's title page is empty, so it must be really good
Something deep and so apocalyptic the secret was held
I think that I'll read it, still, just to know what's in it
But I swear when I finish the last page I won't tell

The house number says triple zero - it must be a dead end address

Though it goes all the way both directions it starts and ends here
The town council tried to get it demolished, but no one voted
They were all in the living room taking in the view

The street sign says 'Hell and Back', so I guess we're already here
We've reached the end of the galaxy - its limits were posted fictitiously
There's no point in leaving unless you're already gone
Whether in mind or body or in some other sphere far beyond

The Stranger, Loner, And Hangman

I don't know which one of these things will become what I desire or need
The rebels and liars become prophets when honest men's integrity bleeds
I can't predict what you'll see, the angel or beggar in me
Both of them are almost the same if you believe anything I say

I question the ways of the times that seem out of step with my rhythm
We don't sync up or speak the same language - it's better that way in a state of schism
I fly away and far in conditions like this, holding the staff
When the podium belongs to these voices I feel no urge to sing along

I'm a drifter on the tracks, micromanaged, because I dream more than land
Call this a disadvantage and I'll disagree for reasons that plea my insanity
I will claim this role and life gladly, as the alternative shows me no merit
A permanent stranger, loner, and my own hangman - just what I always wanted to be

Mirrors Of One Age Into Another

You've read the words of others, now write the words of yourself
The grass is full of leaves fallen from the trees, the grounds covered with inspiration to pick from
Pick the minds of the learned, the dumb, and the mute with all the pleasure you can
Fill your basket with choice selections with your hands busied at all times

You've heard the language used out loud, now use it for yourself
The air is full of notes, all musical, sung in rhythms off many tongues
Dancing from breeze to breeze the wind blows strands and connections around
Throw your own verses out there for other's hooks to find

You've collected thoughts of others, now catalogue all of your own
The scrolls are full of famous things told to many, to few, to the same

Rolls of parchment, new or old, crisp or yellowed by time, have been canistered
Take up a fragment with space to spare and add yours, it's completely fair

You've seen the bards, whose names became known, move on to different avenues
To take in other views of the same things and sometimes things new
Never lingering on past professions of faith, of philosophy, of others of that kind
Move on just the same and watch from a distance who remembers your name

You've watched the eldest, wisest minds and bodies whose time has come and gone
Given way to what comes next, be it natural, be it worse, be it best
Letting nature take its course, time to pass on with all its grace
Observe them with honor, as you become them, between mirrors of one age into another

Connecting Tail To Tale

Having the words to speak is sometimes a luxury
Luxury comes at a cost we can't afford
Affording the tangible and intangible things we surround ourselves with
With or without them we both thrive and suffer

Adding tails onto kite strings
Stringing together words till they make sense
Sensing what's going on around you at all times
Time flies by all the while

What grounded animals wish they could do
Do unto others as you wish others to do to you
You never know what may come, even of the best intentions
Intentions, like words, being the meekest way to speak

Bringing all we can into the conversation
Conversing with others to make sure we're still here
Here, where everything is much like everywhere else
Else we should miss something or pass it up

In the clouds our heads reside, feet chained to the ground
Grounding random thoughts to dust in the process
Processing a world of material from five different senses
Sensing something is wrong when there's too much to sift through

Being all that we can to be ourselves

Ourselves, no more noteworthy than them
Them that define us by association
Association from our eyes being the weakest proof

If only there was a deeper way of discerning
Discerning truth from lie, fact from legend, science from religion
Religion carrying the torch for the greatest and the worst
Worst case scenarios that seem to take up all the press

Moving forward through it all, no matter what
What's good for you is good for me, too, is it not
Not all that glitters is always gold
Golden stars lighting the way on

If it's worth the journey we'll know in the end
Endings are not always where we stop
Stopping for every roadside attraction detracts from the destination
Destinations changing every moment they're considered

How long will our attention stay focused
Focusing on one thing makes the span widen
Widening our restraints and opening chasms
Chasms spill out and spill over with new points to reason

Never-ending tails shake up more dust than we thought
Thoughts of the lines and prints in beaten paths carry over
Over and over the words play in our heads
Heads filled with wonder always tell the best tales

Parts And Pieces

Scarlett letters do not define the sinner
Though we choose to wear them, afterward, all the same

Shackles and chains don't exemplify the criminal
Though they can never be removed mentally, even once physically

The weight of one's soul lies elsewhere
In a place reachable, but from where we cannot return

The corporeality of one's temporal actions is hardly whole

They have so many holes in them air flows freely

Words from our mouths hardly show our character
Though they help to introduce what you're buying into

Impressions are not as serious and stiff as rigid minds allow them to be
And the first ones, often, need amended by a second

Bones don't necessarily hold us altogether
And broken ones don't always slow down our step

Hearts aren't always as transparent through the looking glass
A second glance will show walls being built as we speak

Minds don't always see clearly as a microscope
Where feelings can step in and lead the blind

Eyes aren't always the best windows to the soul
If backdoors are available somewhere else

Ears don't always pick up all the signals
When words get thrown around like slung mud

Hands don't always grasp the importance of the meaning
When simply restraining an idea won't do

Feet won't always take us where we need to go
If a soul in flight is a faster way there

Joints haven't always bent us with the breeze
When, limb from limb, we sway or are torn apart

Yet, all these parts do as they must and will
So have faith in them to be there as much as they can

Thoughts That Steal Sleep

I believe there is a thief, called Lifespan, stealing my centuries
For I'm lucky to make it to one-hundred and have seen few do so, thus far
I fear not death, but respect it well
Only hoping my name's mentioned in the books of great civilizations

I discovered a bandit, called Time, grabbing up my decades
I look back every year along the way, ten at a time, and feel that I just blinked
In that shutter of eye lids clocks hands and planets spun
I only took noticed when someone felt the need to mention it

I have proof of a villain, called Aging, filching my years
Three hundred and sixty five, or six if we leap, slip away in the turn of our back
A day of birth celebrated seems fleeting
Until we then have another coming, so soon, on its trail

I have suspicions of a miscreant, named Laziness, pilfering my months
For twenty eight to thirty one days rationed is not enough, step by step, to build a legacy
Books of money may be balanced within this portion
But books of legends take much longer to pen

I have no doubt a creeper, named Strain, has been thieving my weeks
For seven days pass too quickly to be distracted so easily
Heading this direction while being pulled elsewhere
Eventually being spun around the center of maze with twelve directions to choose from

And I have fears a bad influence, named Laziness, is embezzling my days
Hours sleeping, whittled and frittered away, are slipping through our fingers
Try as we might strength eventually runs out
Giving way to our most costly underdog of an enemy

There is a burglar, dubbed Sleeplessness, running away with my hours
Where minutes are concerned, the day can't seem to hold enough
Twenty-four seems like a lot till almost eight are slept away
And a datebook doesn't always get followed, but lead

Somewhere a scoundrel, dubbed Distraction, is sneaking of with my minutes
Sixty seems a fair number till a clock's hands start turning
The idea of an idle big brother seems harmless
Till ticks and tocks bring on the pressure to perform

Elsewhere, a pickpocket, dubbed Sluggishness, has been pinching my seconds
For, unfortunately, quickness and deftness do not define the mind of a philosopher
I sometimes wish that I were faster, but accept my consistent pace
I'll get where I'm going to quite steadily, just don't ask me to race

The Visitor That Never (But Does) Come

This is not a sad poem, but rather - dare I say - a joyously, melancholy poem
In the style of Whitman's grassy leaves and Thoreau's Walden on his mind's ponderings

We're all waiting for the visitor that never comes; some of us just do it more
philanthropically
Some, with patience, prepare the house with everything to humbly receive his fellow
Others lavishly weight the place down with excessive earthly goods, defiling the purity of
the personal visit
Yet others live and be as they are and let the perchance visitor see what a man being
himself naturally is

My best visitors are the spirit of great orators and account recorders of words and letters
Our visits, often over lamp-lit evening readings, with tea or a nighttime treat

Other visitors are the faint, unswallowed-up echoes of the notes on my guitar
Played back to telling me that I'm far from alone, solitary, or - heaven help me - lonely
I welcome the voice singing back to me, with me; my own words or those of others
Shining a light on new meanings of the same words I've said over and again many times,
already

Other guests are the sounds of the scratching of my pencil
On the pad and paper where I reflect and make sense of everything

I do not seek miserable bliss in scenes of excessive, overzealous excitement
Finding, rather, greater discoveries of myself and others in relative quietude
Music, moving images, and rushes of tantric life and emotion are wasteful
One might as well pace in circles, feverishly sweating bullets for only to pace and collect
sweat by the clip-load (with nowhere to let off the pent-up, explosive powder)

Yet, other visitors don't even know they've made an appearance to me
From a short, visible distance from a window they are completely oblivious

They gather across the street or peripatetically meander down the sidewalk
Faintly, sometimes, can I overhear a pair's conversation and at the last see lips moving as
proof
Be it man or woman and dog or a more complete human brood, its just as nice
So, I cast my net to glean the leavings of our shared energy, either way

NOTES

111

114

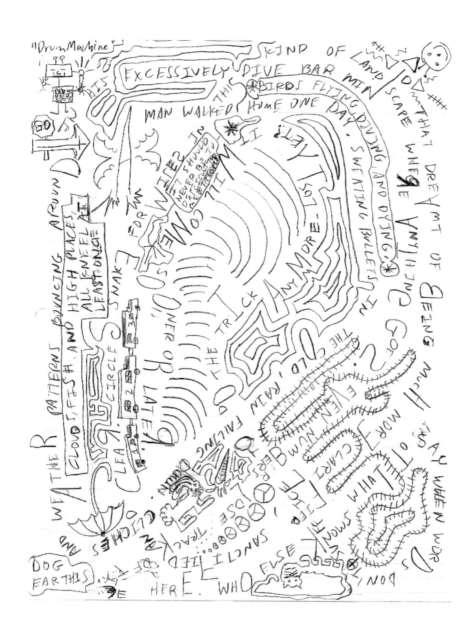

EXCESSIVELY DIVE BAR

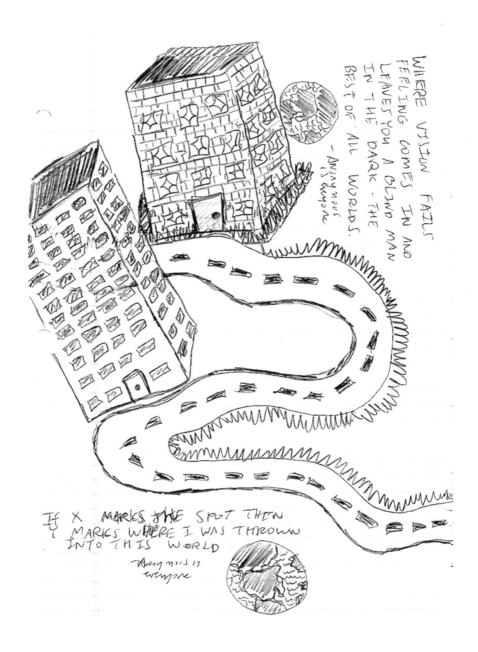

WHERE VISION FAILS
FEELING COMES IN AND
LEAVES YOU A BLIND MAN
IN THE DARK - THE
BEST OF ALL WORLDS.
- Anonymous
is anyone

IF X MARKS THE SPOT THEN
MARKS WHERE I WAS THROWN
INTO THIS WORLD
- Anonymous is
everyone

118

119

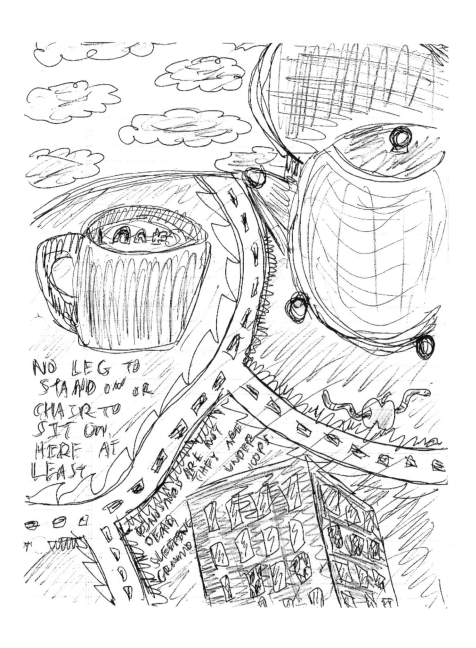

NO LEG TO STAND ON OR CHAIR TO SIT ON, HERE AT LEAST

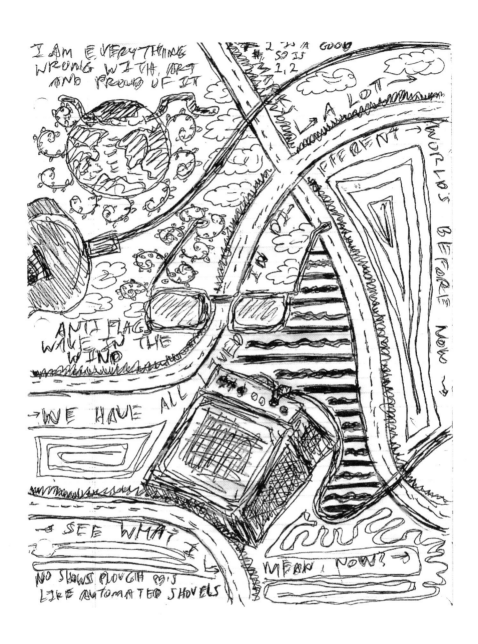

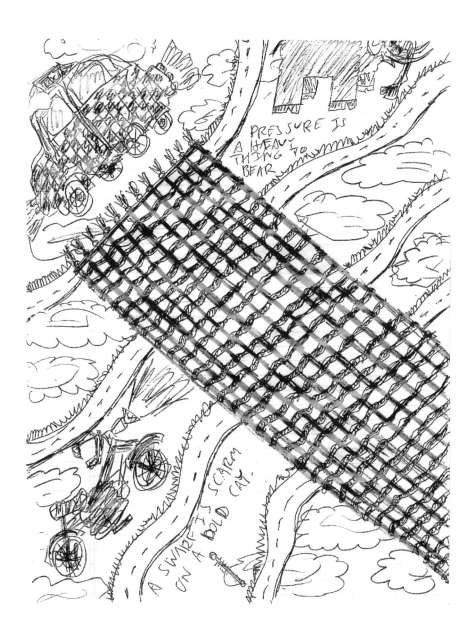

123

If I looked into your eyes would I feel the same
If I took down the names would it come flooding back
When seams become tears do the spaces keep time
When it comes down to this do good reasons exist

If its all built to scale does it tumble and fall
If the signs are in the sky can we reach if we climb
When the ladders extend & getting taller they bend
When the clouds get in the way is there much left to say

"predator"

Every day is so surreal
Concealing nothing, showing everything
I don't believe any of it's real
But it all means everything the same

The details and trivial items trump
All the surface grandeur pales to compare
Such shows of pride are sad and vapid
Nothing's left me impressed, not close

This isn't going anywhere, nor is it
Where's the leg to stand or even a chance
To show conviction or the item on display
Or has it thrown away, again

ZEN
DARKNESS
1H9 IT

I turn to dead poets for inspiration
No living one's have shown to truly commit
The twenty first century seems like a failed experiment
The life has been squeezed out of living art, it's sick

Thanks and Credits:

To my mom for passing her love of the written word in meter and form onto me, and my dad for passing his love of song, structure, theatrical arts, and visual form onto me.

To my brother for his business mind, time, and never-ending efforts to keep me in line and on budget – his practical mind always did offset my dreamer's mind.

To my nephew and niece for their unconditional love, inspiring example, child-like attitude towards the world, and their lovingly bias view of me.

To my grandmother for her unconditional love and support, philosophical and life lessons, external example of grace and pride, and stories of family past.

Thanks to Brian Weir, an old friend who I run into for a few months at a time here and there as fate allows, for being a fellow artist, musician, philosopher, and spiritual guide.

To Father Pahler and Father King for being solid, joyful, yet grounding guides and examples in the ways of faith and spirituality.

To Professor Swaney – especially, of all the professors I've had – for helping me truly appreciate the inner "freak of nature" that makes me stand out.

To anyone and everyone whom I didn't have time or room to mention here, but know who they are and what they've been to me in my life.

NOTES

Michael DeBenedictis is a previously unpublished author. He is 32 years old, and lives in Cuyahoga Falls, OH. When he's not working a day job to pay the bills he pursues a solo music project (Mr. Swan's Song) and poetry projects.

To date his published and distributed works are comprised of multiple albums of original music (from 2009 to current) and this poetry book.

NOTES

Mr. Swan's Poems

By Michael DeBenedictis

ISBN 978-1-312-57670-4

90000

9 781312 576704

CASTING
OFF

Count Christopher de Grabowski

CASTING OFF
Copyright © 2012 by Daisy de Grabowski Richardson

SBN-13: 978-1481247665
ISBN-10: 1481247665

Jacket design by ReyDesign, Boca Raton, FL - reydesign.com

Printed in the U.S.A